13.9.22.

THE CHORALES

THEIR ORIGIN AND INFLUENCE

CHURCH MUSIC MONOGRAPHS

EDITED BY THE REV. H. V. HUGHES, M.A., Precentor of the Society of the Faith

No. 1

THE CHORALES

THEIR ORIGIN AND INFLUENCE

BY

ARCHIBALD W. WILSON, M.A., Mus.Doc.

ORGANIST OF MANCHESTER CATHEDRAL

THE FAITH PRESS, LTD.

22 BUCKINGHAM STREET, CHARING CROSS, W.C. 2

1920

NOTE

THE writer wishes to express his indebtedness to the following works:

WILHELM BAÜMKER: "Das katholische deutsche Kirchenlied in seinen Singweisen."

FRANZ M. BÖHME: "Altdeutsches Liederbuch."

W. H. FRERE: Historical edition of "Hymns Ancient and Modern."

OTTO KADE: "Wittembergisch geistlich Gesangbuch von 1524; neue Partitur-Ausgabe."

H. A. KÖSTLIN: Pamphlet entitled, "Luther als der Vater des evangelischen Kirchengesanges."

C. HUBERT H. PARRY: "Oxford History of Music," Vol. III., and "J. S. Bach."

A. SCHWEITZER: "J. S. Bach" (translated by Mr. Ernest Newman).

PH. SPITTA: "The Life of Bach."

PH. WOLFRUM: "Die Entstehung und erste Entwickelung des deutschen evangelischen Kirchenliedes in musikalischer Beziehung."

JOHANNES ZAHN: "Die Melodien."

FRIEDRICH ZELLE: "Das älteste lutherische Haus-Gesangbuch" and three pamphlets entitled, "Die Singweisen der ältesten evangelischen Lieder."

v

CONTENTS

PART I

THE GENERAL HISTORY OF THE CHORALES

PART II

THE MELODIES WITH HISTORICAL NOTES

THE CHORALES

PART I
THE GENERAL HISTORY OF THE CHORALES

THE INFLUENCE OF THE CHORALES ON GERMAN MUSIC

" I WISH," wrote Luther to his friend Spalatin, " to make German hymns for the people, that the Word of God may dwell in their hearts by means of song also." These words and many other passages in his writings show what immense importance Luther attached to music as an aid to religion. Here he asks of the art a new service : he looks to the popular hymn not only to bring a warmer devotion into public worship itself, but also, and especially, to be a great moral force in the daily life of the home. Böhme[1] tells us how this hope was fulfilled. " Luther's psalms and hymns," he says, " were circulated far and wide. The church song now became also the popular song. The hymns resounded early and late, amid the affairs of business, in every street and market-place." The first Evangelical[2] hymn-books were published in the year 1524, and the movement thus initiated gathered force with the most remarkable rapidity. We may almost say that the making of hymns at once became part of the national life. Bäumker quotes a passage from the preface to Wizel's " Kirchengesänge " of 1546, which says that " throughout half Germany there is scarcely a pastor or a shoemaker who lacks the skill to make a little song or two to sing at church with his neighbours." This popular enthusiasm greatly affected the course of musical development. German music, like German poetry, became devoted to the service of the Church. Both arts were, in Schweitzer's phrase, " impelled upon the religious path." The chorales exercised their influence in two ways.

[1] See his " Altdeutsches Liederbuch," Introduction, p. xliv.
[2] The term " Evangelical " is equivalent to " Lutheran," the Lutheran Church being termed " Evangelical," and the other Protestant Churches " Reformed."

3

First, they were a great moral force, inspiring musicians with high ideals. By means of these simple and beautiful hymns the spiritual fervour which created them was preserved and transmitted from generation to generation. A nation's characteristics are reflected in its music. Thus we find the art sincere and elevated, dedicated to the service of religion. " In the seventeenth century," says Sir Hubert Parry,[1] "the motive that lies behind all the most interesting work of German composers is religious sentiment and fervour." " From the chorale," says another writer,[2] " is derived that almost stern idealism in music which is met with in the works of all the specifically German composers, from Prätorius, Heinrich Schütz, and Johann Sebastian Bach to Johannes Brahms.

Secondly, to the manifold treatment of the chorale melodies is largely due the very remarkable growth of musical technique during the seventeenth century.

In tracing the influence of the chorale on the development of harmony we may take as our starting-point the year 1586, when Osiander, Preacher at the Würtemberg Court, published his " Fifty Spiritual Songs for four voices, set in such a way that the whole Christian congregation can join in them." This work is of great importance as being the first one designed to unite the singing of the choir with that of the congregation. The earlier chorale books had not this double purpose. They fall into two classes : there are the enchiridions, the music of which consists of the melody only, and the polyphonic hymn-books in which the melody, placed in the tenor part, is set contrapuntally for three, four, or five voices. The former were intended only for the congregation, the latter only for the trained choir. Osiander's is the first real hymn-book in the modern sense. The melody lies in the soprano part, where it can be easily recognized, and the accompanying parts move with it, note against note, enforcing its rhythm. It is clear that this style of part-writing involves the homophonic, or harmonic, principle. Its essential feature is the succession of chords, which is the underlying principle of harmony, as

---

[1] " The Oxford History of Music," vol. iii., p. 411.

[2] Köstlin, in his essay, " Luther als der Vater des evangelischen Kirchengesänges," p. 27.

opposed to that of counterpoint, which is the combination of melodic figures. Osiander's work exercised a wide influence. Nearly all the important hymn-books brought out by the great masters of choral music in the early part of the seventeenth century profess the same principles. In the prefaces we read that the melodies have been "simply set,"[1] or "set in contrapuncto simplici, nota contra notam,"[2] or "correctly placed in the soprano part."[3] "Of tunes simply but effectively harmonized," says Sir Hubert Parry, "there are good examples in the sixteenth century, and in the early years of the seventeenth century such settings became numerous. It is noteworthy that even in the early examples composers seemed impelled to make the most of the harmonization and voice-parts so as to enhance the expression." In this respect the harmonic settings of Calvisius, Gesius, Eccard, Vulpius, and Prätorius and others, have a kinship with those of J. S. Bach, which occur in his Passion music, his church cantatas, and the large collection published after his death. It is true that during this period the "new music" of Italy was exercising considerable influence on German composers, and, in the natural course of musical development, there was a strong tendency towards homophony. It may, however, be fairly claimed that in the chorale musicians found not only an opportunity for cultivating the homophonic style, but also an incentive to do so. They intended, in these settings, to unite the singing of the congregation with that of the choir, and it was only by means of homophony that this union could possibly be effected.

Not only were the chorale melodies harmonized: they were used also as canti fermi for contrapuntal treatment. The work of this kind done by the German Protestant organists led to results of the greatest importance. From the treatment of these hymn-tunes as the basis of organ preludes there was developed a new style of counterpoint, far more elastic and free, and of far wider range of expression than the old choral counterpoint. To the composition of choralvorspiele[4] the organist composers of the seventeenth century devoted their highest abilities. After Pachelbel and Buxtehude, the greatest of these, came

[1] *v.* Hassler's "Kirchengesänge," of 1608.
[2] *v.* Prätorius' "Musæ Sioniæ," Part VIII., published in 1610.
[3] *v.* Vulpius' "Ein schön geistlich Gesangbuch," of 1609.
[4] Organ preludes based upon a chorale melody.

the greatest of all time, J. S. Bach, to whose poetic nature this form was particularly attractive. In his hands it assumes a new significance, for he treats at the same time both tune and words of the hymn. In his music we have not only a beautiful organ arrangement of the chorale melody, but often also an exquisite tone-picture illustrating the text associated with the melody.

The growth of instrumental polyphony had naturally a great effect upon choral music. In this branch of the art, as in organ music, the hymn-tune is the "golden kernel entangled in a silver tissue of counterpoint." The forms and to a certain extent the texture of organ music were applied to choral works. For instances of this we may turn to Bach's chorale cantatas, the opening choruses of which are mostly framed upon the model of the organ prelude. The scheme is usually either that of the Pachelbel choralvorspiel, in which each line of the melody is treated fugally before it makes its appearance as a canto fermo, or that of the less organic choralvorspiel in which polyphony is woven round the melody without any development of its constituent phrases.

Thus, during the period which began at the Reformation and ended in 1750, we see the rise and growth of a distinctive school of German music upon the foundation of the chorale. The first Evangelical hymn-books were published in 1524. From that date to the death of Bach the chorale melodies run like golden threads through nearly all the finest work of German composers. "In considering what we may call Bach's spiritual ancestry," says Mr. Fuller Maitland,[1] "it would be impossible to lay too much stress on the influence of the chorale upon his training." Brought up on these melodies, Bach turned to them throughout his life with ever increasing love. He composed the chorale prelude on " Wenn wir in höchsten Nöthen sein " (" When we are in deepest need ") just before he died, dictating, it is said, the music to his pupil and son-in-law, Altnikol. With characteristic piety, as he felt death approaching, he altered its title to the words " Vor deinen Thron tret' ich hiemit " (" Before Thy throne I now appear "), which is the first line of a Morning hymn also sung to this melody.

---

[1] " Oxford History of Music," vol. iv., p. 14.

THE HYMN-BOOKS

THE LUTHERAN CHORALE BOOKS

THE origin of the chorale melodies will be considered later. Here, however, it is necessary briefly to mention the main sources from which they are derived.

The melodies may conveniently be classified in four groups. First, there are those of the old German folk-hymns which gradually during the Middle Ages won their way into the services of the Catholic Church. Secondly, there are the melodies which have come from Latin hymns. Here we must distinguish between those which are versions of plainsong melodies and those, quite different in character, which belonged to the later popular Latin hymns. In the third group are the melodies which were originally associated with secular texts. Most of these are genuine folk-tunes: a few, however, were taken from the works of contemporary musicians. Lastly, there are the original melodies, composed, for the most part, when the supply from other sources began to fail. Thus we see that at the Reformation there was already at hand a spiritual song in the popular tongue: the old German folk-hymns were a foundation on which the new hymnody could be built. These folk-hymns Luther set himself to revise, giving them a new poetic beauty and adapting them to the teaching of the Evangelical Church. Many of the Latin hymns had already been translated into German. To these translations, which also he revised, he and his friends added others, at the same time writing a considerable number of original hymns. After the revision of the texts came that of the melodies, the latter receiving in most cases more drastic treatment than the former. The process of adaptation was always in the direction of simplicity of phrase and definiteness of rhythm. In this work Luther had the help of two eminent musicians, Conrad Rupff and Johann Walther, whom

7

in 1524 he summoned as his guests to Wittenberg. Köstlin depicts the three men at work. "While Rupff and Walther," he says, "sat at the table bending over their music sheets, pen in hand, Father Luther paced up and down, trying over on his fife the melodic phrases, which streamed from his memory and imagination to join themselves to the words of the hymn, until at length the tune was firmly established, as a rhythmically complete, well-rounded, strongly compacted whole."

The first three Lutheran hymn-books appeared in 1524. These are the "Etlich Christlich Lider," the "Erfurt Enchiridion," and Johann Walther's "Gesangbüchlein." The "Etlich Christlich Lider," commonly called the "Achtliederbuch," is a collection of eight hymns and four melodies. The "Erfurt Enchiridion," which has twenty-six hymns and ten melodies, is described on its title-page as "A little hand-book useful for a Christian at the present time for the practice of sacred songs." Two editions of it, differing chiefly in the order of the contents, appeared simultaneously, the one printed by Trutebul at his press "The Dyeing Tub" ("Zum Ferbefass"), the other by Maler at "The Black Horn" ("Zum Scharzen Horn"). The "Achtliederbuch" and the "Erfurt Enchiridion" were intended primarily for home use. The music of both consists of the melodies only. In Walther's "Gesangbüchlein," on the other hand, the melodies are set polyphonically for three, four, and five voices. This work, which was intended for the trained choir, did not appear in score: only the separate voice-parts were printed.

It has generally been supposed that of these hymn-books the "Achtliederbuch" is the earliest. Zelle, however, is of opinion that it was published after the other two. It was probably edited by Paul Speratus, the author of several well-known hymns, three of which it contains.

The relation between the "Erfurt Enchiridion" and Walther's "Gesangbüchlein" has been much discussed by German hymnologists. The following account of the subject is mainly taken from Zelle's "Das älteste lutherische Haus-Gesangbuch":—

As soon as Luther and his friends had finished their texts, Walther began to set them to polyphonic music for the school choirs, established in connection with certain churches for the singing of the music of the liturgical service. Some of these hymns, either with the melody only or with the whole polyphonic setting, appeared as broadsheets in 1523. The next step was to make the hymns known to the people, and for this it was necessary to publish them in book-form with the melodies only. A choice was therefore made out of Walther's collection of those hymns which were most suitable for a popular hymn-book. The melodies which were too elaborate were simplified, and those which were unsatisfactory as unison songs were replaced by others. Further, for the sake of simplicity, two hymns were often set to the same melody. It was probably Luther himself who undertook this work. The editing of the book, however, he entrusted to his friend Justus Jonas, who took the hymns with him to Erfurt and had them published simultaneously at the presses of Trutebul and Maler. Thus, the " Gesangbüchlein " is the earlier work, and, indeed, the basis of the " Enchiridion." The " Enchiridion " was probably, however, the first to be published. The fact that Luther's preface occurs in the " Gesang-büchlein " and not in the " Enchiridion," until later editions, suggests that the preface was not ready when the first edition of the " Enchiridion " was printed.

We have seen with what enthusiasm the hymns were received. Not only were new editions of the " Erfurt Enchiridion " quickly issued, but there appeared also within a few years numerous other hymn-books which were based upon it. As many of these were unauthorized by Luther and contained pirated and inaccurate reprints of his hymns, he thought it wise to prepare a new and authoritative unison hymn-book, which, entitled " Geistliche Lieder auff new gebessert " (" Spiritual Songs recently improved "), was published probably in 1529. In the preface Luther wrote : " Because I see that the more often our first hymns are printed, the more inaccurate they become, I beg and admonish all no more to improve upon and augment our little book." Only a few pages of this hymn-book are now extant and we have to learn of its contents from later editions. The first of these, namely, Klug's Gesangbuch of 1529, is also lost, but its contents were printed in the " Journal von und für Deutschland " of 1788. Another edition was brought out by Andreas Rauscher in 1531 at Erfurt. This too has been lost, but only within recent years. There used to be a copy of it in the Library at Helmstedt: Wackernagel quotes from it, but Zahn could not find it there. Klug's Gesangbuch of 1535 and that of 1543, Schumann's of 1539, and Babst's of 1545 are also in the main reprints of Luther's "Geistliche Lieder." Babst's Gesangbuch is the last hymn-book that was brought out under Luther's direction. For this Luther wrote a new preface, his third. The book appeared in two parts and contains a hundred and twenty-nine texts and ninety-seven hymn-tunes. It was reissued several times and remained the authoritative Evangelical hymn-book till the end of the century.

Five editions of Walther's " Gesangbüchlein " appeared during the author's lifetime: published in 1524, it was reissued in 1525, 1537, 1544 and 1551.

The hymn-books of the Reformed[1] Churches will be considered later. One of them, however, calls for mention here, in that it is of German origin and contains several of Luther's hymns. The " Deutsch Kirchenamt . . . wie es die Gemeinde zu Strassburg singt " (" The German Service . . . as sung by the congregation at Strassburg ") was published in 1525. It was edited by Matthäus Greiter and Wolfgang Dachstein, who, before they espoused the cause of the Reformation in 1524, were monks attached to Strassburg Cathedral, Greiter as a singer, Dachstein as Organist. Here appeared for the first time the two famous melodies, " Es sind doch selig alle die," better known as " O Mensch bewein' dein' Sünde gross'," and " An Wasserflüssen Babylon," the former composed probably by Greiter, the latter, almost certainly, by Dachstein. This book is no longer extant: the only remaining copy was burnt at the siege of Strassburg in 1870. Fortunately, however, a reprint of it in facsimile had been issued in 1848. Its contents were included in the " Psalmen, Gebett und Kirchenübung," brought out at Strassburg in 1526, which book is now the earliest extant source of the two melodies.

It has already been said that the early chorale books are of two kinds. There are those in which the melodies are presented in a unisonous form and those in which they are set polyphonically. The polyphonic settings were intended for the trained choir. The canto

[1] The term denotes those Protestant Churches other than the Lutheran (Evangelical) Church.

fermo lies in the tenor part and the counterpoint is often elaborate. The enchiridions, or unison hymn-books, were intended primarily for home use. Luther wished the hymns first to take root in the home, purposing to introduce them later, when they were well known, into the Evangelical service. Catharine Zell, the Strassburg reformer, in the preface to her "Gesangbüchlein," expresses the hope "that, if at night the crying child has to be rocked to sleep, the mother may sing it a song of heavenly things." We now come to a new phase in the history of Lutheran hymnody. Like so many of the important stages in the development of the chorale, it was initiated, not by a professional musician, but by a priest. In 1586 Lucas Osiander, Preacher at the Court of Würtemburg, published his "Fifty Spiritual Songs, set for four voices in such a way that the whole Christian congregation can join in them." In the preface he explains his aim and his method. The former is "to enable a layman, uninstructed in figured music, to join in the singing of the choir": the latter is to remove the melody to the soprano part, where it can be easily recognized, and to make the accompanying parts move with it in the simplest species of counterpoint, note against note. Osiander's work is the first in which the settings of the melodies are definitely homophonic: it is thus the prototype of the modern hymn-book. The principles laid down by Osiander were widely adopted. They underlie most of the numerous collections of chorale settings brought out at the end of the sixteenth and the beginning of the seventeenth century. The most important of these are the following: Calvisius' "Harmonia Cantionum Ecclesiasticarum" and Eccard's "Geistliche Lieder auf den Choral," published in 1597: Gesius' "Geistliche deutsche Lieder" of 1601; Hassler's "Kirchengesänge mit vier Stimmen simpliciter gesetzet" of 1608; Vulpius' "Ein schön geistlich Gesangbuch" of 1609; and the nine volumes of the "Musae Sioniae" of Michael Prätorius, published 1605-1610. Schweitzer, however, warns us against supposing that these great masters of church music were mere imitators of Osiander. They were following, not only the lead of the Würtemberg Court Preacher, but also a natural tendency in music towards the development of homophony.

"The really creative period of the hymn," says Schweitzer, "begins at the end of the sixteenth century." We may conveniently date it from the publication in 1598 of Philipp Nicolai's religious treatise, entitled " Freuden Spiegel des ewigen Lebens " (" Mirror of the Joys of the Life Eternal "). Here, in an appendix containing four hymns, are first found the famous " Wachet auf! ruft uns die Stimme " and " Wie schön leuchtet der Morgenstern," together with their superb melodies. The most copious hymn-writers of the seventeenth century were Johann Heermann, author of " Herzliebster Jesu was hast du verbrochen," and Johann Rist. Of Rist's six hundred hymns only some five or six have survived. He brought out his " Himmlische Lieder " in 1641 and 1642, with the help of his friend Johann Schop, who composed most of the melodies. The period of the Thirty Years War, which devastated Germany from 1618 to 1648, was a time of great outpouring of sacred poetry. " The war," says Miss Winkworth, [1] " caused religious men to look away from the world " : the soul of the nation took refuge in the chorale. The hymns became more and more the expression of deep personal feeling. Of this subjective character are the hymns of Johann Franck (1618-1677), the author of the beautiful " Jesu meine Freude " and " Schmücke dich o liebe Seele," and those of his great contemporary, Paul Gerhardt—by universal consent the " prince of Lutheran poets "—who wrote a hundred and twenty hymns, among which are " O Haupt voll Blut und Wunden," " Befiehl' du deine Wege," and " Nun ruhen alle Wälder."

The sacred poetry of the seventeenth century could not fail to inspire the musicians of the time, as in later years it inspired Bach. " There was hardly an Evangelical musician of this period," says Schweitzer, " who did not compose melodies for the church." Among all writers of hymn-tunes Johann Crüger holds the foremost place. No other has enriched the service with so many fine congregational melodies. His first hymn-book, " Newes vollkömliches Gesangbuch," was published in 1640. In his " Geistliche Kirchen-Melodien " of 1649 the melodies are harmonized for four voices, with obligato parts for violin and cornet. The date of his most important work, the famous " Praxis Pietatis Melica," which in 1703 had already reached its thirtieth edition, is doubtful. The first, second, and fourth editions

[1] See " Christian Singers of Germany."

are lost. We know, however, from a remark in the preface to the "Kirchen-Melodien," that the third edition was published in 1648 and there is still extant a defective copy of the hymn-book which in all probability belongs to this edition. The earliest extant complete copy belongs to the fifth edition, brought out in 1653. In the " Praxis Pietatis Melica " the melodies are arranged simply, with only a figured bass to indicate the harmony. Crüger's work marks the climax of the great classical epoch of chorale creation: his death in 1662 marks the beginning of its decline, and the end of the century its conclusion.

It is true that the eighteenth and nineteenth centuries witnessed the production of a vast amount of hymns. A full account of those of the Pietistic period (1680-1757)[1] and those of the Rationalistic period (1757-1817) is to be found in the Rev. James Mearns' able article in the " Dictionary of Hymnology." " The spirit, however," as Schweitzer says, " which dominated music about the beginning of the eighteenth century made it incapable of developing the true church tune any further. German music got out of touch with German song and fell further and further under the influence of the more 'artistic' Italian melody. It could no longer achieve that naïveté which ever since the Middle Ages had endowed it with those splendid, unique tunes." Bach's own hymn-tunes are a case in point : exquisitely beautiful, they are, however, sacred arias rather than congregational melodies. Most of them were first published in Schemelli's " Musicalisches Gesangbuch " of 1736, a hymn-book the melodies of which Bach himself selected and arranged with a figured bass. It is probable that twenty-one of these melodies were composed by Bach, though only one of them actually bears his name.

In the foregoing survey only the leading features of the subject have been touched upon. The number of chorale books that appeared during the two centuries under discussion is indeed countless. The period was one of intense religious feeling and the means by which the spiritual fervour of the people found expression—the key that unlocked

[1] Freylinghausen's "Geistreiches Gesangbuch," published in 1704, may be mentioned as an especially important hymn-book of this period. Von Winterfeld attempted to show that Bach had a share in its production, as musical editor, but this view is definitely rejected by Spitta.

the nation's heart—was the hymn.   Each generation and all classes of
the people helped to swell the national treasury of sacred song.   The
" Erfurt Enchiridion " contains twenty-six hymns : the eight volumes
of the " Andäctigen Seelen geistliches Brand-und-Gantz Opfer " (" The
whole spiritual burnt-offerings of devout souls "), published at Leipzig
in 1697, contains over five thousand.   A special interest attaches
to this latter hymn-book.   We know that Bach possessed it, for its
name occurs in the inventory of his property, which was made at
his death.

THE HUGUENOT PSALTER

Calvin was born at Noyon in Picardy in the year 1509.   In 1533, as
a supporter of the Reformation, he was obliged to leave Paris.   Three
years later he went to Geneva, whence, however, he was soon " driven
away "[1] by a storm of opposition that his severity had raised.   From
1539 to 1541 he lived at Strassburg, as Pastor of the French Reformed
Community.   Here, in 1539, he published his first psalter, entitled
" Aulcuns Pseaulmes et Cantiques mys en chant."   The texts of this
small book consist chiefly of the first twelve of Marot's metrical psalms
and some of Calvin's own.   Of its twenty-one melodies only nine, one
of which is Greiter's " Es sind doch selig alle die," were retained in the
subsequent psalters.   In 1541 Calvin returned to Geneva, where he
remained till his death in 1564.

At Geneva he brought out several psalters, the earlier psalms of
which were mainly 'the work of Clément Marot, the later ones being
written by Théodore Beza.   In the preparation of these psalters Calvin
had for some years the help of Louis Bourgeois, a musician of great
ability, whom the Genevan Consistory appointed Cantor of one of the
churches.

The psalm-tunes fall into two groups.   The first, and by far the
finer group, consists of the eighty-five melodies that appeared up to
1551.[2]   These, the nine melodies of the Strassburg psalter excepted,

[1] " Bientôt chassé de Genève, où son rigorisme trouvait une vive opposition."
Douen, " Le Psautier Huguenot."

[2] There were melodies for eighty-three psalm versions and the metrical versions
of the Commandments and *Nunc Dimittis* that were appended to them.

were either composed or adapted by Bourgeois. It is not known who is responsible for the second group, which comprises the forty new melodies to Beza's psalms, that appeared in the complete psalter of 1562.

Calvin's views on church music differed in one important respect from those of Luther. Luther, who wished "that all the arts should be used for the glory of Him who created them," gave the warmest encouragement to polyphonic music. Calvin, however, refused to sanction it: to him such "frills of popery" were unworthy of the sanctuary. It was on this point that there arose between Calvin and Bourgeois a difference that led finally to a complete rupture. Bourgeois wished to introduce part-music into public worship, and with this view published arrangements of the psalm-tunes in four-part harmony. The Genevan Church, however, forbade the use of such settings and in 1557 Bourgeois left Geneva and returned to Paris.

The complete French psalter, "a master-work to which all nations that foster an Evangelical church song are indebted,"[1] was published in 1562, and it was not long before its tunes, many of which had already been incorporated in English psalmody, appeared set to psalm versions in nearly every European language. From the early years of the Reformation, verse translations and paraphrases of certain psalms had been in use in Germany. Besides those hymns of Luther himself which are based on psalms, there may be mentioned Dachser's psalter of 1538, and that of Waldis, published in 1553. The most important German psalter, however, is that of Dr. Ambrosius Lobwasser, Professor of Law at Königsberg, who as early as 1565 had completed a German translation of the French psalm versions and adapted his texts to the hundred and twenty-five melodies of the French work. Lobwasser's psalter remained in manuscript for eight years, being first printed in 1573. The French psalm-tunes then became known in Germany, and many of them soon found their way into the Lutheran hymn-books. Among the chorale melodies which thus came from the French psalter, there are three of particular importance. These are "Freu' dich sehr o liebe Seele," "Herr Gott dich loben alle wir" (known in England as

---

[1] Douen, p. 735.

the " Old Hundredth "), and " Wenn wir in höchsten Nöthen sein."
The first two appeared in the Genevan psalter of 1551, and the third in
the psalter of 1547, published at Lyons.

THE HYMN-BOOKS OF THE BOHEMIAN BRETHREN

The Union of the Bohemian Brethren, or " Unitas Fratrum," which
was founded about 1467, soon after the Hussite revival, arose out of
certain religious communities of Bohemia and Moravia which from
early times had points of difference in use and doctrine from the
Roman Church, and later became wholly independent. At the Reformation it seemed likely that the Brethren might join themselves to the
German Evangelical Church. We know that Luther had a warm
friendship for them : " I cannot regard them," he wrote, " otherwise than as my brothers." The union between the two Churches
was, however, never effected, and after Luther's death their mutual
goodwill gave place to colder feelings.

Vernacular hymn-books were in use among the Bohemian Brethren
at an early date. One of these, belonging to the year 1501, is still
preserved in the Museum at Prague : another, the Bohemian " Can-
tional " of 1505, is, however, lost.

In 1531, Michael Weisse, leader of the German members of the
" Unitas Fratrum," brought out a German hymn-book entitled " Ein
new Gesengbuchlen." This collection of a hundred and fifty-seven
texts, and a hundred and twelve melodies, the former comprising
translations both from Latin and Bohemian, as well as original hymns,
at once attracted considerable attention in Protestant Germany, and
much of its contents, both words and music, soon became incorporated
in the Lutheran chorale books. The most important chorales borrowed
from Weisse's hymn-book are those which are German versions of late
Latin hymns, adapted to their original melodies. Two of these may
be especially mentioned, namely, " Christus der uns selig macht," and
" Menschenkind merk' eben," the former being a translation of " Patris
Sapientia," the later of " Ave Hierarchia." The melodies of both
occur several times in Bach's works.

Another important hymn-book of the Bohemian Brethren is Bishop Johann Horn's " Ein Gesangbuch der Brüder in Behemen und Merherrn," published in 1544. It comprises most of the melodies of Weisse's book together with twenty-four others. Here for the first time we find the melody " Menschenkind merk' eben " associated with what has proved its permanent text, namely, Horn's own hymn " Gottes Sohn ist kommen."

GERMAN CATHOLIC HYMN-BOOKS

Mention has already been made of the German folk-hymns which gradually during the Middle Ages won their way into the service of the Catholic Church. " This growing stream of Teutonic hymnody," says Dr. Frere, " in time divided into four channels." From this original source are derived, to a varying extent, the hymnodies of the Lutheran and German Reformed Churches and the Church of the Bohemian Brethren, while " the Catholic flow went on in a narrowed and conservative channel." The subsequent development of vernacular hymnody that took place in the Lutheran Church was, as we have seen, both great and rapid. That in the Catholic Church, on the other hand, was comparatively small and of later date. It may be said generally of the Catholic hymn-books, that though they contain many fine chorale melodies of their own, some original and some which the Church herself adapted from ancient sources,[1] they are, however, largely indebted in respect of their music to the Lutheran hymn-books.

In the first half of the sixteenth century there was little in the way of vernacular hymns available for Catholic use, but quite a small collection, entitled "Ein new Gesangbüchlin Geistlicher Lieder," brought out by Vehe in 1537. Later in the century, however, Johann Leisentritt, Dean of Budissin, did much to further the cause of congregational singing in the Catholic Church by bringing out three hymn-books on a much larger scale. The first of these appeared in 1567, the other two

[1] The notation of the beautiful melody " Es ist ein' Ros' entsprungen " is first found in the " Alte Catholische Geistliche Kirchengesang " of 1599.

in 1573 and 1584. Another hymn-book that calls for mention is
the Andernach " Catholische Geistliche Gesänge " of 1608. Like the
preceding, it contained hymns in Latin with German versions, as well
as original German hymns. Here the plainsong melodies of the Latin
hymns are for the most part discarded and replaced by tunes of the
chorale type. Some of these, being serviceable though of no great
distinction, are still in use.

LUTHER AND WALTHER

LUTHER was born at Eisleben in 1483. His early childhood was spent amid the poor and coarse surroundings of German peasant life. For some years he attended St. George's School at Eisenach. As a "poor student" he had certain privileges: he paid no school fees, received free lodging in a hospice, and was allowed to beg for his bread at the house-doors of the town, in return for which he sang as a chorister in the church connected with the school. While at Eisenach, he attracted the attention of the wife of a rich merchant, Frau Cotta, who took him into her household. In 1501 Luther went to Erfurt and for four years attended its famous University. He then entered the Convent of the Augustinian Eremites at Erfurt and, after due novitiate, became a monk. In 1508 he was sent to Wittenberg to assist the University which had recently been opened there. After a mission to Rome, he returned to Wittenberg and was made a member of the Senate. Here Luther began his work as a Reformer. On November 1, 1517, he nailed his ninety-nine theses against Indulgences on the door of the Schloss-kirche. He now became leader of the German revolt against Rome. After attending the Diet at Worms, to which he was summoned to make his defence, he retired for safety to the Wartburg at Eisenach.

It was after his departure from the Wartburg in 1522 that Luther began to occupy himself with projects for the reform of the services of the church, which led to such important musical results. In 1523 appeared the " Formula Missæ," in which he raises objection to certain parts of the Mass. He forbids the long Graduals, allowing only two verses and the Alleluia ; the Offertorium ; with a few exceptions, the Sequences ; and " for the present," the Introits (" though the psalms from which they are taken are dear to us "). He touches upon the subject of vernacular hymns. "I wish," he says, "that we had many German hymns which the people might sing in the Mass, with the Gradual, the Sanctus and Agnus Dei: for who can doubt that the hymns,[1] which the choir now sing alone, were formerly sung by the whole church?" The pastor of the church, he says, could arrange either that these German hymns should be sung immediately after the Latin ones, or that the Latin and German hymns should be sung on alternate days. "But," he adds, "we lack German poets and musicians (or they are unknown to us) who are capable of writing Christian and spiritual songs worthy of being sung daily in the church of God." Luther then goes on to recommend that, while the people are receiving the Holy Sacrament, the old German hymn "Gott sei gelobet und gebenedeiet" should be sung, but "without the later unscriptural additions"; he mentions also "the beautiful Christian hymn 'Nun bitten wir den heiligen Geist.'"

Luther had long cherished the idea of a German Mass and in 1524 summoned Conrad Rupff and Johann Walther to Wittenberg to help him to arrange the music. The "Deutsche Messe und Ordnung des Gottesdienstes zu Wittenberg fürgenommen" was published in 1526. Here several German hymns are appointed to be sung: one at the beginning of the service instead of the Introit; at the Epistle "Nun bitten wir den heiligen Geist"; after the Gospel the German Credo "Wir glauben all' an einem Gott"; at the Administration the German Sanctus "Jesaja dem Propheten das geschah" or "Gott sei gelobet und gebenedeiet" or Huss's hymn "Jesus Christus unser Heiland," and the German Agnus Dei "Christe du Lamm Gottes."

Side by side with the German Mass Luther retained the Latin Mass, partly for the sake of the young who might otherwise grow up ignorant of the Latin language and partly because the time was not ripe for a strict uniformity.

There are many proofs of Luther's lifelong love of music. We read in his "Tischreden" ("Table-talk"): "I always loved music; whoso has skill in this art is of a good temperament and fitted for all things. We must teach music in the schools: a schoolmaster ought to have skill in music, or I would not regard him: neither should we

---

[1] *I.e.*, the choral portions of the Latin Mass.

ordain young men as preachers unless they have been well exercised in music." And again: " Music is one of the best arts: the notes give life to the text. Kings and princes ought to maintain music: we are told in the Bible that the good and godly kings maintained and paid singers." In his so-called " Lobrede auf die Musik "—a preface, originally written in Latin, to Johann Walther's " Lob und Preis der himmlischen Kunst Musica "—Luther most admirably describes the wonders of polyphony. " When natural music," he says, " is heightened and polished by art, there man first beholds, and can with great wonder examine to a certain extent (for it cannot be wholly seized or understood), the great and perfect wisdom of God in His marvellous work of music, in which this is most singular and indeed astonishing, that one man sings a simple tune or tenor (as musicians call it) together with which three, four, or five voices also sing, which as it were play and skip delightedly round this simple tune or tenor and wonderfully grace and adorn the said tune with manifold devices and sounds, performing as it were a heavenly dance, so that those who at all understand it and are moved by it must be greatly amazed, and believe that there is nothing more extraordinary in the world than such a song adorned with many voices."[1]

Luther, as a young man, practised music with great diligence and enthusiasm. He played the flute and the lute, and sang, the soprano voice of the Eisenach chorister having changed to a " fine counter-tenor." We are told that he and his friends used to meet for the practise of part-singing. He had a special regard for the motets of Josquin des Près. Of him he once said, " He is the master of the notes: they do as he wills: other composers do as the notes will." Many proofs of Luther's great admiration for plainsong and folk-music are to be found in the chorale books. The melodies of three hymns in the " Erfurt Enchiridion " are based upon plainsong melodies: Luther's own " Ein' feste Burg " is, in Schweitzer's phrase, " woven out of Gregorian reminiscences." At the Reformation also many secular tunes, from the mountains, the streets and the taverns, were admitted into the service of the church. " The devil," said Luther," does not

---

[1] From Schweitzer's " J. S. Bach " (translated by Mr. Ernest Newman), vol. i., p. 29.

need all the good tunes for himself." The melody "Herr Christ der einig Gotts Sohn," No. X. in the "Erfurt Enchiridion," is of secular origin, and for his own Christmas hymn, "Vom Himmel hoch da komm' ich her," Luther chose the tune of a popular riddle-song, which, however, he had later to discard, as it still continued to haunt "every dancing-booth and tavern."

We now come to a question that has been much debated by German hymnologists : To what extent was Luther, theologian and poet, also a composer ? Undoubtedly most of the new melodies to Luther's hymns were composed either by Luther himself, or by Walther, or by both in collaboration. The above question therefore involves another, for we cannot estimate the position of Luther, as a writer of hymn-tunes, without reference to that of Walther. It will be convenient to deal now with both questions together.

That Luther had sufficient musical capacity to write hymn-tunes and, indeed, did actually take part in providing music for the Evangelical service, is beyond doubt. Michael Prätorius in his "Syntagma Musicum" prints a statement made by Walther, that it was Luther himself who set the Epistle, Gospel and Sacramental Words to musical inflections for the "Deutsche Messe" of 1526. We know also that Luther wrote a melody (which, however, did not satisfy him) for his hymn "Vater unser im Himmelreich." Von Winterfeld, in his edition of Luther's hymns, gives the facsimile of a manuscript in Luther's writing, which shows, in conjunction with a preliminary draft of the words, a crossed-out sketch for a corresponding melody.

There is little or no direct evidence to show which of the new melodies to Luther's hymns are Luther's, and which were composed by Walther : we must seek a solution of the problem chiefly in the conditions under which the melodies first appeared and, in one or two cases, in the build of melody itself. We may make use of two general principles. The first is, that if we have no ground for supposing the contrary, we may reasonably attribute the melodies, first found set polyphonically, to the composer of the setting. The second is that, subject to the same condition, we may reasonably attribute the melodies, first found in a unisonous form, when we have knowledge of his musical capacity, to the author of the text. In applying these two principles we occasionally come across rival claims between polyphonist and poet (as now, in the case of Luther and Walther), owing to the fact that the same melody appeared simultaneously both in a unisonous form and set polyphonically. It is here claimed that in such cases the balance of probability inclines to the polyphonist. He is the expert musician, and as we know that the polyphony is his, we may assume, if there is no evidence to contradict it, that the melody is his also.

Of the melodies under consideration the most important that first appeared in a unisonous form are " Ein' feste Burg," " Jesaja dem Propheten das geschah," and " Vom Himmel hoch da komm' ich her."[1] These were in all probability composed by Luther. Zelle, it is true, raises a doubt about "Vom Himmel hoch." The text, which is Luther's "sacred parody" of the folk-song "Aus fremden Landen komm' ich her," was set to three melodies. The first, that of the original folk-song, Luther discarded. The second, here attributed to Luther, is the splendid melody frequently found in Bach's works, and still in general use. The third was written by Walther. It is certainly remarkable, as Zelle points out, that, if Luther wrote the second melody, Walther, his friend and colleague, should have written another to supersede it. The point, however, is a small one and is outweighed by other considerations. The last line of the second melody is identical with that of " Ein' feste Burg." Again, we have reason to believe that when Luther could not find a tune for his hymns, he entrusted the task to Walther ; in other words, that when the melodies to Luther's hymns are not the work of Walther, they are mostly due, as original or adapted, to Luther himself. But Walther can hardly be the composer here, as it is most improbable that he would have written the third melody if he had already written the second, which is by far the finer.

There can be no doubt that Luther was to a certain extent indebted to plainsong for his melodies. " Ein' feste Burg " and " Jesaja dem

[1] The well-known melody, first found in Klug's Gesangbuch of 1535 where it is set to Luther's hymn, " Nun freut euch liebe Christen g'mein," set later to " Es ist gewisslich an der Zeit," and associated in English hymnals with the hymn "Great God, what do I see and hear ?" (see " Hymns Ancient and Modern," No. 52) is not included, as it is generally supposed to be of secular origin. There is a story that Luther heard it on a journey, and noted it down.

Propheten das geschah " contain lines which clearly were suggested by the music of the Roman Gradual. We may reasonably assume that the plagiarism, if plagiarism it can be called, was unintentional and due to the fact that Luther was unconsciously employing the musical phraseology with which he happened to be most familiar. The subject has been discussed by Catholic and Protestant writers in rather a partisan spirit. "In early times," says Wolfrum, "an ardent but blind enthusiasm led people to attribute to Luther nearly all the melodies that were set to his texts, and certain foolish admirers even went so far as to call him the Palestrina of the Protestant Church : for this," he adds, "modern criticism has taken a bitter revenge, in that Catholic writers, such as Meister and Baümker, maintain that he did no more than put a few melodies together out of plainsong phrases, and Protestant writers unfortunately think themselves obliged to acquiesce in this verdict." This statement, in regard to modern opinion about Luther's indebtedness to plainsong, needs considerable qualification, for a close examination will show a wide difference between the views held by Meister and Baümker and those of Köstlin, Zahn, Schweitzer and others. Baümker analyzes "Ein' feste Burg" and "Jesaja dem Propheten das geschah" line by line and quotes the plainsong passages from which, he asserts, these melodies are derived. He certainly implies, if he does not actually state, that Luther selected and made use of these passages with deliberate intent. Köstlin, on the other hand, ridicules the idea that "Ein' feste Burg" was "put together like a musical mosaic." "These Gregorian motives," he says, "occurred spontaneously to the Eisenach choir-boy of former days' trained in the music of the Catholic Church, and what Luther has created out of these scattered fragments is something new and original, a German song, whose characteristic physiognomy and animating force are Luther's own work." Zahn, in his note on "Ein' feste Burg," states his opinion as follows. "Baümker," he says, "sought to prove that the melody was taken from the Roman Gradual : but the resemblance between the phrases which he found there scattered about in different places and the lines of the hymn-tune is only such as could be found in older music for any melody." The best opinion on the subject may be summed up in Schweitzer's words. "Ein' feste Burg," he says, "is woven out of Gregorian reminiscences. The recognition of this fact," he adds, "deprives the melody of none of its beauty and Luther of none of the credit for it : it really takes considerable talent to create an organic unity out of fragments."

The new melodies to Luther's hymns, which appeared in Walther's "Gesangbüchlein" of 1524, were probably composed by Walther himself, the author of the polyphonic setting. Among these are " Aus tiefer Noth schrei' ich zu dir " (the Phrygian melody), " Ein neues Lied wir heben an," " Es woll' uns Gott genädig sein " (better known by its later text, " Christ unser Herr zum Jordan kam "), " Mit Fried' und Freud' ich fahr' dahin," and " Nun freut euch liebe Christen g'mein."[1] Wolfrum, it is true, attributes " Ein neues Lied wir heben an " to Luther ; he does so mainly for two reasons : first, because it is written in the key of F (the " modus lascivus "), which seems to have been the key that Luther particularly liked ; secondly, because its opening phrase resembles that of " Ein' feste Burg," which Luther wrote five years later. The first point is a small one : Luther had no monopoly of the key of F ; Walther also often employed it. Nor need we attach much importance to the second point, for in Walther's setting of the " Deus misereatur "—one of the five Latin texts of the "Gesangbüchlein "—there is a phrase (in a different key, it is true) which resembles the first line of " Ein' feste Burg " more closely than the opening of " Ein neues Lied " does. As Walther certainly wrote the more similar phrase, he may well have written also the less similar one. We may, however, make a distinction between those melodies of the " Gesangbüchlein " which occur also in the " Erfurt Enchiridion " of 1524, namely, " Ein neues Lied " and " Aus tiefer Noth," and those melodies which do not so occur, namely, " Es woll' uns Gott genädig sein," " Mit Fried' und Freud'," and " Nun freut euch," and say that the latter are more probably Walther's than the former. We have this additional reason for attributing " Es woll' uns Gott genädig sein," " Mit Fried' und Freud'," and " Nun freut euch " to Walther : it may be argued that they probably are not Luther's, because, unless he had wanted them for the " Erfurt Enchiridion "—the hymn-

---

[1] This is the first of the two well-known melodies that were set to the text. The second one, first found in Klug's Gesangbuch of 1535, is usually known as " Es ist gewisslich an der Zeit," or (in English hymnals) as " Great God, what do I see and hear ?"

book which he himself was preparing—he would not, under the stress of his manifold activities, have spent time over the writing of them. Walther's " Gesangbüchlein " was reissued several times, and probably most of the new melodies found in these later editions are his work.

We may reasonably assign to Walther a very high place among the melodists of the Evangelical Church. Modern opinion certainly favours such an assumption. We cannot doubt that in early times Luther's position as a melodist was rated too high and Walther's too low. Now, after fifty years of critical study of the chorale melodies, Luther's reputation as a composer rests on but a few hymn-tunes, one of them, however, of great excellence and another which is among the finest in all hymnody. Walther's reputation has necessarily increased, for there is no reason for attributing the new melodies to Luther's hymns, which we find in the " Gesangbüchlein," or simultaneously in the " Gesangbüchlein " and the " Erfurt Enchiridion," to anyone else than Luther or Walther. We may trace the stages in this change of opinion. It does not seem even to have occurred to Von Winterfeld, whose book " Der evangelische kirchengesang " was published in 1843, that Walther himself might have composed the canti fermi of his polyphonic settings: those of the melodies in question which he does not attribute to Luther he is content to leave anonymous. Wacker-nagel, a few years later, admits the probability that some three or four melodies were written by Walther. Kade in his " Neue Partitur-Ausgabe "[1] of the " Gesangbüchlein," published in 1878, argues at some length to prove that " Ein neues Lied " and " Mit Fried' und Freud' " should be added to this number, and hints at the general conclusion reached by *Zelle* in his pamphlets of 1899, 1900 and 1910, namely, that the new melodies to Luther's hymns which first appeared in Walther's " Gesangbüchlein," or simultaneously in that collection and the " Erfurt Enchiridion," may much more reasonably be attributed to Walther himself, the expert and undoubted author of the polyphony, than to Luther.

Luther died in 1546, and was buried at Wittenberg in the Schloss-Kirche, on the door of which some thirty years before he had nailed his theses against the Roman Indulgences. His greatest hymn, " Ein' feste Burg ist unser Gott," was sung over his grave.

[1] " New Edition in Score."

Johann Walther was born in the year 1496 at a village near Cola (perhaps the modern Kahla near Rudolstadt) in Thuringia. About 1523 he entered the Precentory of Frederick, Electoral Prince of Saxony, at Torgau. At first a bass singer, he was soon promoted to more important positions. In 1525 he succeeded Rupff as "Electoral Singing-master of Saxony," and, in a letter dated 1526, Melanchthon speaks of him as "Composer in the precentory." When in 1530 the prince through lack of funds gave up his precentory at Torgau, Walther, encouraged by Luther, organized a new precentory maintained by the Torgau Corporation. In 1547 Walther went as Kapellmeister to the Court of Prince Moritz of Saxony, in Dresden, where he remained till 1554. He then retired with a pension to Torgau, where he died in 1570. Under his portrait in the family vault were inscribed the hexameters:

> " Non tam dulce melos caneres, Walthere magister,
>   ni tecum caneret simul et spirabile numen."

> (" *Thou wouldst not have sung so sweet a melody, O Walther, master,*
>   *had not God sung with thee and inspired thee.*")

Kade in his "Neue Partitur-Ausgabe" of Walther's "Gesang-büchlein" gives an interesting account of the composer's life and work. He claims for him, both as a polyphonist and melodist, a high place among musicians of his time.

The polyphonic settings of the "Gesangbüchlein" fall, according to their style, into two classes. First, there are the simple settings, in which the voices enter together and the first species of counterpoint (known as "note against note") is largely employed. Here Walther has adopted the style hitherto chiefly associated with secular part-music. Kade emphasizes this point. He says that this was Walther's most notable service to church music, and attributes to his influence the later homophonic settings of the chorale melodies made by Osiander, Calvisius, Hassler and others. He points out, however, the difference between their work and Walther's. With but one exception, Walther places the melody in the tenor part. Again, he does not clearly mark the line-divisions of the hymn: it is only at the beginning of the first line that the voices always enter together. Secondly, there are the elaborate settings, which abound in variety of figure and such artistic devices as imitation and canon.   Walther's work is undoubtedly unequal : among much that is dull, the harmonies being empty and the progressions harsh, are found settings of remarkable beauty and polish. Perhaps the two finest examples of the simple style are " Mit Fried' und Freud'" and "Aus tiefer Noth," the former, with its beautiful cantus fermus and its smooth, melodious counterpoint, being a master-piece of delicate workmanship.   The finest examples of the elaborate style are " Nun bitten wir den heiligen Geist " and " Gott der Vater wohn' uns bei," both of which are written in five-part polyphony: of these Kade says that " they are unequalled in the whole literature of the time."

The work of Luther and Walther marks the beginning of a new era in the history of music.   In itself a great musical achievement, it is, however, primarily important as a great moral force influencing German national life and, in consequence, German music.   What the relations between these two pioneers were we may safely conjecture. Luther, reformer, poet, theologian and musical amateur with flashes of genius, evolved the true principles of the popular church song, not only expounding them by word, but embodying them in his own texts and melodies.   The idea of the congregational hymn, by means of which "the Word of God might dwell in the hearts of the people," being fixed in their memory by the magical tenacity of song, was his great concep-tion; the power to carry it out in its entirety he derived from Walther. Luther had but little time to give to church music, high though he rated its importance.   In Walther he found his ideal colleague : the expert musician, with his ready faculty for acting upon suggestions ; the composer, with his gift of melodic invention ; the contrapuntist, who, in the cause of establishing the chorale, could enkindle the enthusiasm and enlist the co-operation of the trained choir.   We have already seen with what feelings of emotion these hymns were received. The time was ripe for them.   They gave expression to a deep and widespread religious sentiment.   Moreover, as they enshrined so they preserved this sentiment, which, handed on from generation to genera-tion, remained the animating motive of German music for more than two centuries.

THE

ORIGIN OF THE CHORALE MELODIES

THE chorale melodies are the growth of many centuries. Their history, even if we leave out of account those which are based upon plainsong, goes back far into the Middle Ages. Five centuries lie between " Christ ist erstanden " and Crüger's " Nun danket alle Gott." They represent, moreover, diverse melodic types, for among them there are many drawn from the rich store of secular song. Some of these are old folk-tunes, sprung from the people, loved and sung by generation after generation: others the Reformers borrowed from the works of contemporary composers. The most important chorale melody in Bach's " St. Matthew Passion " was composed for a love-song. Nor are they all of German origin. The beautiful " Was mein Gott will das g'scheh' allzeit " and several others came from France ; the gay, almost rollicking " In dir ist Freude " from Italy. "Any melody," says Schweitzer, " which had charm and beauty was stopped at the frontier and pressed into the service of the Evangelical Church." Thus, in order to trace the origin of the chorale melodies, we must take a wide survey of musical history.

We meet with many difficulties, the consideration of which may well form a preface to the subject. They arise chiefly in connection with the melodies of the early chorale books. What we know of these is almost entirely due to research, for very seldom do the hymn-books themselves give us any information about them. Many of these melodies, it has been ascertained, come from the old German folk-hymns, from Latin hymns, and from secular folk-song. These sources, however, are too obscure to admit of a thorough investigation : a fuller knowledge might show that there are also other melodies which are derived from them.

Of the melodies that cannot be traced to pre-Reformation times a few perhaps may be old ones that have not been verified, but the majority, no doubt, were expressly written for the Evangelical service. With regard to the latter we have two problems before us.

The first is to ascertain whether the melody is wholly new, or in part based upon some other. The Reformers made use of old melodies in two ways. Not only did they borrow from ancient sources a great number of melodies in their entirety, but they made considerable use of old melodic fragments in the composition of their otherwise new melodies. How wide this partial use of old melodies was, it is impossible to say. On the one hand a melody may be based upon some unknown model : on the other hand, a resemblance between one melody and another may be purely accidental. There are, however, certain well-authenticated instances of it. The chief source made use of in this partial way is plainsong, Luther's " Ein' feste Burg " and " Jesaja dem Propheten das geschah," and Decius' " Allein Gott in der Höh' sei Ehr'," which is based on the first phrases of an old Easter Gloria (" Gloria Paschalis "), being cases in point. Catholic hymnologists lay great stress on this indebtedness of Evangelical hymnody to plainsong. They are, however, probably overstating their case when they trace the first lines of " Wachet auf " and " O Lamm Gottes unschuldig " to the first five notes of the fifth Gregorian tone : such a phrase may surely be considered common property. Melodic fragments were borrowed also from other sources. Walther's " Christ lag in Todesbanden " is partly based upon phrases from the twelfth century " Christ ist erstanden," and the first two lines of " Wie schön leuchtet der Morgenstern " are identical with those of an older melody, " Jauchzet dem Herren alle Land."

What is the explanation of this partial use of old melodies ? We cannot doubt that in some cases these phrases were borrowed and incorporated in the new melodies intentionally. It can hardly be accidental that Decius' melody for his German Gloria, " Allein Gott in der Höh' sei Ehr'," is largely composed of phrases from the " Gloria Paschalis." Again, Luther, in the " Erfurt Enchiridion," heads his text " Christ lag in Todesbanden " with the title " Christ ist erstanden, gebessert (improved)," from which we may safely assume that its melody also was purposely based on that of the twelfth-century hymn.

But in other cases, that of "Ein' feste Burg" for instance, these borrowed phrases appear to be reminiscences rather than copies, and it is probable that the composer was quite unconscious of any plagiarism. It must be remembered that many of the Reformers had been brought up in the singing-schools of the Catholic Church and thus, being familiar from childhood with plainsong, they would naturally in composing their melodies make use of its idiom.

The second problem is to assign these new melodies to their author. In this connection two general principles of investigation have already been mentioned.[1] The first is that, if we have no ground for supposing the contrary, we may reasonably attribute the melodies first found set polyphonically to the composer of the polyphony. The second is that, subject to the same condition, we may reasonably attribute the melodies first found in a unisonous form, when we have knowledge of his musical ability, to the author of the text. The latter principle, however, can only be applied in comparatively few cases, for in most we do not know whether the writer of the words was musical or not. Consequently the authorship of many of these melodies must remain doubtful. Such, for instance, is the case with "Wachet auf! ruft uns die Stimme" and "Wie schön leuchtet der Morgenstern." We cannot feel sure that they were composed by Philipp Nicolai, the author of the texts, for we do not know that he had musical ability : we can only say that we have no ground for attributing them to anyone else.

We may classify the chorale melodies in four groups. First, there are the melodies that come from the German hymns of the Middle Ages. In the second group are the melodies derived from Latin hymns. Here we must distinguish between three main original types, namely, the plainsong melodies, the Sequence melodies and the melodies of the Latin hymns of the fourteenth and fifteenth centuries. The third group consists of the melodies which were originally associated with secular texts. Lastly, there are the melodies which were expressly written for the Evangelical service.

[1] See p. 22.

I.—THE GERMAN HYMNS OF THE MIDDLE AGES

With the conversion of Germany to Christianity came the introduction of the Roman Liturgy and the Gregorian music. "Among the nations of Europe," says Johannes Diaconus, "it was the Gauls and the Germans who applied themselves most diligently to the task of learning the new song." After this meed of praise the chronicler continues in a different strain and we read as follows : "They had, however, the fault that they could not leave the music intact: out of frivolity they were wont to mingle with it snatches of their own songs. There was, too, their natural roughness to contend with. Strong of body, they possessed powerful voices, and the modulations which they heard they could not reproduce in a delicate manner. Indeed, with their throats made hoarse by strong drink, their singing degenerated into a natural roar, like the noise of a heavy waggon rolling down the mountain side, so that the listener was more stunned than moved to devotion." Evidently the musicians who had to teach the people the song of the Church became discouraged and began to shirk their duty, for in 759 Bishop Chrodegang of Metz issued the following order: "If there be found any teachers so arrogant as to refuse to impart to others the art which they by the Grace of God possess, they shall be severely punished." In time the people learnt the Latin song, but it still remained foreign to their nature. They had an irresistible impulse to express their devotional feelings in their own tongue. The Church, however, at first regarded vernacular hymns with disfavour. Pope Charles the Great forbade them "on account of the roughness of the German language." He had, however, the cause of church music much at heart, and wishing to encourage the people to take part in the singing of the Latin song, he ordained in his Capitular of 789 that "the people shall sing the Doxology, and the Priests, together with the people and the Holy Angels, shall sing the Sanctus." The song of the Responds was added to the people's share by Ludwig II. in 856.

In considering the origin of German sacred song and its introduction into the services of the church, we must attach the greatest importance to a custom which arose at a very early date and soon obtained the widest currency. It is alluded to in the Statutes of Salzburg of 799, which ordain that "the people shall learn to sing the 'Kyrie-eleison,' and that too, not in such a disorderly way as heretofore, but better." Some time before this date the words "Kyrie-eleis" had become a popular religious cry in which the people gave vent to their pent-up feelings. It was sung on all possible religious occasions: at funerals, during pilgrimages, on the battlefield, at the reception of high church dignitaries and the enthronement of bishops. Nor was it confined to public ceremonies: "the peasant," says Baümker, "sang it behind his plough, the carpenter at his bench, and the sick man on his bed." In this way a great number of tunes came into being, for the words were not, in the main, used as an isolated ejaculation, but, being repeated or drawn out by long vocalizations on each syllable, formed, as it were, the text of several connected musical phrases. The music, we may assume, was largely based on the plainsong of the "Kyrie-eleison" which the people heard in church. In the course of time, these tunes, for their better preservation, were revised and provided with German texts, the verses of which always ended with the refrain "Kyrie-eleis." Such hymns were called "Kirleisen" or Kyrie-songs.

The oldest extant Kyrie-song is a hymn to St. Peter, which belongs to the ninth century. There is a copy of it in the Royal Library at Munich: the melody, however, which is written in neumes, has so far proved undecipherable. By the twelfth century the use of German hymns had become common among the people. In 1148 Gerhoh, the Prior of Reichersperger, in his Commentary on the Psalms, writes: "The whole world sings the praises of the Saviour, in songs, too, in the mother tongue: chiefly is this the case with the Germans, whose speech is the best fitted for well-sounding songs." There is the evidence also of the monk Gottfried, who accompanied St. Bernard on his mission along the banks of the Rhine in 1146. "After we had left German territory," he says, "the song 'Christe uns genade' was no more heard, and there was no one then who could sing songs to God." He adds that the Roman people had no songs in their own tongue, like the songs of the Germans, "wherein they can give thanks to God for all His marvels." The chorale books contain many of these old

Kirleisen.[1] The most notable, on account of its immense popularity in the Middle Ages, is the twelfth-century Easter hymn "Christ ist erstanden." It is mentioned frequently in early manuscripts, and the beginning of it is found in nearly all the Latin Office-books printed in Germany between 1480 and 1522. This hymn more than any other "helped to conquer the Church" and win her favour for German sacred song. To the same period belongs the Whitsuntide hymn "Nun bitten wir den heiligen Geist." It is mentioned in a thirteenth-century manuscript of a sermon preached by Brother Berthold of Ratisbon. We read there : "It is a useful song : the more you sing it, the more you love it. He was a wise man who wrote it." In most cases the Lutheran Church adopted both text and melody of the medieval folk-hymns ; occasionally, however, only the melody was utilized. For instance, the text of the first hymn in the "Erfurt Enchiridion" is Luther's paraphrase of the Ten Commandments, "Dies sind die heil'gen zehn Gebot'," and the melody, as the super-scription informs us, is that of the twelfth-century Pilgrim's song, "In Gottes Namen fahren wir."

The Mystery Plays, which had so great a vogue in the fourteenth and fifteenth centuries, did much to foster the growth of German sacred song. It was customary for these sacred dramas to take place at Christmas, Passiontide, and Easter. Especially beloved by the people were the representations of the Christmas Story, and the cradle-songs, which were the most popular feature of these, have still quite an irresistible charm. The oldest of these cradle-songs come from the latter part of the fourteenth century. To this period belong the Latin-German Mischlied "In dulci jubilo," "Puer natus in Bethlehem" (though its German version, "Ein kind gebor'n zu Bethlehem," may be a little later) and "Joseph lieber Joseph mein." The last named is a Wechselgesang or Rotation-song, its verses being allotted in turn to different characters. In the first verse the Blessed Virgin asks

---

[1] The term is here used broadly to denote the old German hymns the verses of which end with the refrain "kyrie-eleis." According to Baümker the melodies of the hymns "Christ ist erstanden" and "Nun bitten wir den heiligen Geist" are founded respectively on those of the Sequences, "Victimæ Paschali laudes" and "Veni Sancte Spiritus," in which case the two hymns cannot strictly be called Kirleisen.

Joseph to help her to rock the cradle; in the second verse Joseph expresses his readiness to do so; then follow verses for the choir and the children who are present.

Several important German hymns are first found in the fifteenth century, though some of them probably are of earlier origin. "Wir glauben all' an einen Gott," with its melody, first occurs in a Breslau manuscript of 1417. Above the German text runs a Latin one, "Credo in Deum patrem omnipotentem," which, according to Baümker, is an "Interpolation" or "Trope" to the liturgical Credo. At the Reformation the melody was adapted to Luther's "German Credo," likewise beginning "Wir glauben all' an einen Gott." The hymn (the text only) of the Seven Words "Da Jesus an dem Kreuze stund" first appears in a fifteenth-century Vienna manuscript. Baümker, however, points out that the word "stund" implies an earlier date and assigns the hymn to the fourteenth century—a time when it was still customary, in representations of the Crucifixion, to depict the Saviour with His feet supported on a foot-rest.

We now come to the question of the Church's general attitude towards vernacular hymns. Undoubtedly she warmly encouraged their use in her extra-liturgical services. We have seen that German hymns were sung at the Mystery Plays, and a great many other religious ceremonies organized by the Church. On the other hand, the Church kept careful guard lest vernacular hymns should become a regular part of her liturgical service, though in concession to strong popular feeling she sanctioned their use on a few special occasions. "German sacred song," says Schweitzer, "gained admission into the religious service of the Church under cover of the Kyrie and the Alleluia." It seems that at these parts of the liturgy the people were allowed on the great festivals to introduce German verses which had, however, something of a liturgical character, in that they always ended with the refrain "Kyrie-eleis" or "Alleluia." Again, in certain Dioceses the people were allowed to sing a German hymn with the Sequence. Thus, after "Victimæ Paschali laudes" would follow the Easter hymn "Christ ist erstanden"; after "Grates nunc omnes," the Christmas hymn "Gelobet seist du Jesu Christ." The Schwerin Ordinarium of 1519 gives the following direction: "On Christmas Day the choir, kneeling, shall sing the Sequence three times. In the meanwhile the Celebrant shall take the Holy Sacrament and present it to the people for adoration: thereupon these shall sing three times the Canticum Vulgare, 'Gelobet seist du Jesu Christ.'" Occasionally, also, German hymns were sung before and after the sermon.

"The German Reformation," says Schweitzer, "had this advantage over the French, that it found a spiritual song already existing in the popular tongue and therefore a ground on which it might build." If we compare the chorale melodies which are derived from this source with those derived from secular folk-song, it will strike us that on the whole the sacred melodies are the older. They certainly bear the marks of greater antiquity. It may be, however, that the secular folk-tunes are of equally early origin, but in the course of time have lost something of their ancient character. Such tunes were subject to constant change. They lived on the lips of the individual whose taste, fancy, and skill had a large share in determining their form. Each generation, so to speak, brought them up to date, refashioning them according to the idiom of the age. The sacred folk-tunes were guarded against this by being used in public worship. No doubt different localities had their different uses, for it is true that in certain cases we find several forms of the melody. The fact, however, remains that by belonging, not to the individual but to the congregation, they were in the main preserved from arbitrary variation.

II.—THE MELODIES WHICH THE EVANGELICAL CHURCH BORROWED FROM LATIN HYMNS

The melodies now about to be considered represent, in their original form, widely different types. On the one hand there are those which are derived from the old plainsong melodies and, on the other hand, there are the melodies of the popular Latin hymns of the fourteenth and fifteenth centuries which, entirely loosed from the Gregorian tradition, approximate to folk-song. Between these two types, but on the whole nearer to the second, are the Sequence melodies. In the chorale books, however, this original diversity of character largely disappears, for the old plainsong melodies, with their free rhythm and melismatic ornamentation, have undergone a process of simplification and have been remoulded into a popular form.

German translations of Latin hymns date from a very early period. It is probable that the oldest, which belong to the eighth century, were not intended to be sung, but were written merely to elucidate the Latin text. To the twelfth century Baümker assigns translations of the hymns " Veni, Creator Spiritus," " Veni, Redemptor Gentium," " Ave praeclara Maris Stella " and others, which, he assumes, were sung to simplified versions of the old melodies. Of special importance is the work of Johannes, Monk of Salzburg, in the fourteenth century : his numerous translations of Latin hymns into the vernacular did much to foster the growth of German sacred song. Thus at the Reformation there were already at hand German versions of most of the well-known Latin hymns. Some of these needed but little revision before their incorporation in the chorale books, and others served as models for new versions. It is evident that Luther had in mind the old translation of " Veni, Creator Spiritus " when he wrote his own translation, " Komm' Gott Schöpfer heiliger Geist," for in both there occurs the rhyming phrase " wie (als) du weist " though there is nothing in the original to suggest it.

" It is unthinkable," says Köstlin, " that so broad-minded a man as Luther, who, moreover, was familiar from childhood with the Romish church song, would have rejected, out of opposition to the Romish Church and the whole Romish system, even its fine melodies." " The rich treasure of Gregorian song," he adds, " was the earliest source from which Luther drew." The " Erfurt Enchiridion " contains three hymns derived from this source, namely, " Nun komm' der Heiden Heiland," " Christum wir sollen loben schon," and " Komm' Gott Schöpfer heiliger Geist." These are respectively translations of the Latin hymns "Veni, Redemptor Gentium," ascribed to St. Ambrose, " A solis ortus cardine," written by Sedulius in the fifth century, and " Veni, Creator Spiritus," ascribed to St. Gregory the Great or to Rabanus Maurus (died 856), and their melodies are popular versions of the original plainsong. By comparing the Lutheran form of these and other melodies of the same type with the originals we see the adapter's aim and method. His aim was to make of the old melody an easy, popular congregational hymn-tune: his method was to simplify its progressions and to give it a clearly defined rhythm. The treatment was often drastic. The main outline of the original is indeed always reproduced in the new form which we find in the chorale books, but, in most cases, two very characteristic features of the old music wholly disappear. By the substitution of single notes for the melismata (groups of notes sung to one syllable), the old melodies were shorn of their graces of ornamentation: by being brought into strict time they lost their rhythmic freedom and variety. But the purpose of the adaptation was most successfully achieved. We have in the Lutheran version of these old plainsong melodies congregational hymn-tunes both popular and dignified, of simple phraseology and well-defined rhythm.

Other chorales, with their melodies, come from the Latin Sequences. Perhaps the most prominent are " Danksagen wir alle " and " Als der gütige Gott "—the former a translation of the Sequence, " Grates nunc omnes," the latter a translation of " Mittit ad virginem." It is true that even these are only of minor importance, but they occur frequently in the sixteenth-century chorale books, and the latter, in Crüger's abbreviated and more rhythmical form, is well suited to congregational use. The origin of the Sequences is to be found in the old " Jubilations " or Tropes, which may be defined as vocalized[1] musical phrases interpolated in, or added to, the Gregorian music of the Church. An early mention of this habit of ornamentation occurs in a passage in the writings of St. Augustine. It runs as follows: " The singers, inspired to holy joy at first by the text of the song, were soon stirred to such deep emotion, that they could no longer express by means of words what they felt in their innermost being. They therefore put words aside and poured forth their feelings in a Jubilation. The Jubilation is a song which gives vent to the soaring of the heart that cannot be expressed in words. And to whom is such a song more due than to the Highest Inexpressible Being ? " We are here concerned mainly, if not only, with the Jubilations on the final syllable of the Alleluia which was sung on Festivals just before the Gospel at Mass. At a later date these were revised and provided with Latin texts, such songs being

---

[1] *I.e.*, sung to a single vowel sound.

called Sequences[1] or Proses. The oldest Sequences date from the ninth century and are those which Notker Balbulus, in the course of his work in the singing-school of the monastery of St. Gall, in part collected and in part himself arranged.

In the case of the melodies of the late Latin hymns very little alteration was necessary to adapt them to the needs of the Evangelical Church. They had already, in the simple, tuneful character of their original form, the main elements of popularity. They belong to the folk-song type. They have the same measured, clearly marked rhythm, and the majority of them are in the Ionian mode transposed to F—the " modus lascivus," so-called from its predominance in secular tunes. Wolfrum writes as follows : " The love of song, which so marks the fourteenth and fifteenth centuries, gave rise to a great number of Latin folk-hymns. The peripatetic monks, in particular, composed and sang many hymns in the popular Latin with which they were familiar. These verses show the naïvely religious character of the people and may, with their melodies, be regarded as folk-songs. In many cases, doubtless, the Latin text is a translation of the original German one." Three of these late Latin hymns have especial importance in the history of the chorale, namely, " Patris Sapienta," " Ave Hierarchia," " Dies est lætitiæ." Their melodies, in connection with the chorales " Christus der uns selig macht," " Menschenkind merk' eben," and " Der Tag der ist so freudenreich," which are respectively translations of the three Latin texts, became well known in the Evangelical Church, and are found also in Bach's works.[2] The hymn " Menschenkind merk' eben," however, gradually fell out of use and, in Bach's time, the melody was commonly associated with the hymn " Gottes Sohn ist kommen."

[1] The Sequence was so named because it followed on after the Alleluia. Perhaps also the name was influenced by the formula for the announcing of the Gospel, " Sequentia Sancti Evangelii secundum . . .," etc. (See " Hymns Ancient and Modern," Historical Edition, Introduction.)

[2] See the organ arrangements of these melodies in Bach's " Orgelbüchlein." The melodies " Christus der uns selig macht " and " Menschenkind merk' eben " occur also elsewhere in Bach's works.

III.—THE CHORALE MELODIES ORIGINALLY ASSO-CIATED WITH SECULAR TEXTS

Schweitzer well says that " all true and deeply felt music has its home on the heights where art and religion dwell." Nowhere do we see the truth of this more plainly than in the chorale books. The most important chorale melody in the "St. Matthew Passion" was composed by Leo Hassler for the love-song " Mein G'müt ist mir verwirret." Bach has introduced it no less than five times, and its occurrences mark the supreme moments in the sacred narrative. In the same work also are the chorale melodies " O Welt ich muss dich lassen " and " Was mein Gott will das g'scheh' allzeit," the former of which originally belonged to the folk-song " Insbruck ich muss dich lassen," and the latter to the little French love-song " Il me suffit de tous mes maux." Two of these melodies are, to-day, among the best-known and most beloved in all hymnody. Destined for immortality, they were not long confined to the narrow limits of their original texts. Twelve years after its first appearance we find the melody " Mein G'müt is mir verwirret " set to Knoll's Funeral hymn " Herzlich thut mich verlangen," with which, and with Gerhardt's Passion hymn " O Haupt voll Blut and Wunden," it is still associated. " There is no other melody," says Spitta, " that Bach used so frequently or more thoroughly exhausted as to its harmonic possibilities for every variety of purpose." " In the hymn-books of the missionaries," says Böhme, " it has gone the round of the world." " Insbruck ich muss dich lassen " is first found about 1475. It came into sacred use as early as 1505 in association with a hymn to SS. Anna and Joachim, and was set later both to Hesse's Funeral hymn " O Welt ich muss dich lassen " and Gerhardt's Evening hymn " Nun ruhen alle Wälder." Böhme concludes his historical note on the melody as follows: " So has this simple German tune lived its life. Created, it may be, on the high-road by workmen sad at leaving their native town, it has been sung in the church and in the home, on occasions both of joy and sorrow, and played at evening from the church tower by cornet and tower-horn, and is still, after four hundred years, one of the most beloved of hymn-tunes."

The Reformers made abundant use of secular melodies. There was, in the first place, the special need of popular music for the Evangelical service. "A true instinct," says Köstlin, "told them that there was nothing profane in the melody itself, provided that, when set to good, sacred words, it no longer carried with it any suggestion of its original text." This condition, however, was not always fulfilled. We know, for instance, that Luther found it necessary to discard the folk-tune "Aus fremden Landen komm' ich her," the reason, no doubt, being, as Böhme was the first to point out, that it still retained its popularity in the dancing-place and tavern. He was compelled, in Schweitzer's words, "to let the devil have the tune back again," and to replace it with another—the splendid melody, probably Luther's own, which has ever since been associated with his Christmas hymn.[1] This was not the only failure. Other tunes disappeared from the chorale books for similar reasons. Among the many, however, that retained their place are some of the most beautiful and devotional melodies in the whole treasury of sacred song. "Who thinks," says Köstlin, "when he hears the melodies 'Nun ruhen alle Wälder' and 'Herzlich thut mich verlangen' that the one originally belonged to the song of the itinerant artisans, 'Insbruck ich muss dich lassen,' and that the other was composed by Hassler for a love-song? Who, when he sings the rather sombre 'Kommt her zu mir spricht Gottes Sohn,' is reminded of the fact that the melody is no other than the old 'Lindenschmittston,' which, set to countless songs, was widely popular in South Germany, and sung everywhere—in the street, in the spinning-room, and at the drinking-bout?'

To secure suitable hymn-tunes for the church service was not the Reformers' only concern: they had in view a wider purpose. They sought, by supplying the well-known secular tunes with edifying words, to elevate popular music in general. In a collection of songs brought out at Frankfurt in 1571 we read on the title-page as follows: "Street songs, Cavalier songs and Mountain songs, transformed into Christian and moral songs, for the abolishing in course of time of the bad and vexatious practice of singing idle and shameful songs in the streets, in the fields and at home, by substituting for them good, sacred, honest words." This use of secular tunes for educational purposes was not an entirely new idea at the Reformation. Examples of it are to be found

[1] *I.e.,* "Vom Himmel hoch da komm' ich her."

in the previous century. In folk-song the production of tunes never kept pace with that of texts. A popular tune often did duty for several songs, new words being written for the old music. With the object of utilizing folk-song as a means of religious instruction, the tunes were sometimes provided with " sacred parodies" of their original texts—sacred verses not only reproducing the metre of the folk-verses, but also employing, in many cases, similar turns of phrase. The earliest hymns of this kind are those written between 1415 and 1443 by Von Loufenberg, Dean of Freiburg in Breisgau. Several " sacred parodies" are to be found among the hymns of the Reformation. Luther's " Vom Himmel hoch da komm' ich her " is modelled upon the folk-song " Aus fremden Landen komm' ich her," and Hesse's " O Welt ich muss dich lassen " upon the Wanderlied " Insbruck ich muss dich lassen," both hymns appearing set to the original folk-tunes. Roughly speaking, we may say that the secular melody won its way into the services of the church by means of the " sacred parody."

The first secular tune that we find in the chorale books is " Mein' Freud' möcht' sich wohl mehren "; it occurs, set to the hymn " Herr Christ der einig Gotts Sohn," both in the " Erfurt Enchiridion " and Walther's " Gesangbüchlein." Of the later instances of this conversion of secular tunes to sacred use the following are important : In 1544 the French tune " Il me suffit de tous mes maux " (already mentioned) was set to the chorale " Was mein Gott will das g'scheh' allzeit," and in 1570 the tune of the hunting-song " Einmal thät ich spazieren " to " Von Gott will ich nicht lassen." In 1591 the Italian Gastoldi published his five-part madrigal " A lieta vita Amor c' invita," the melody of which afterwards became " In dir ist Freude." The folk-tune " Es ist auf Erd' kein schwerer Leid'n " is found printed with the hymn " Ich hab' mein' Sach' Gott heimgestellt " (" I have committed my affairs to God ") in 1609, though it seems that they were associated together some years before this. Finally, as one of the latest instances, there is the chorale " Eins ist Noth ach Herr," the melody of which comes from the Halle students' drinking-song. The latter part of it, indeed, is rather suggestive of its origin, " recalling to some extent the time when the young men sang it over their glass of beer."[1]

[1] Köstlin.

If, on the one hand, there were some chorale melodies of secular origin which, owing to their power of profane suggestion, had to be discarded, there are, on the other, some which won the day over melodies especially composed for the church. " Durch Adam's Fall ist ganz verderbt " is a case in point. Walther's " Gesangbüchlein " has two melodies for the text. Both of these, however, fell out of use as soon as a third melody, the one in present use, appeared in Klug's Gesangbuch of 1535. The origin of this last was not known until Böhme found proof that it is the so-called " Pavier-ton "—a tune frequently mentioned during the sixteenth century, belonging to a song about the Battle of Pavia which took place in 1525.

It has already been stated that Lutheran hymnody owes several of its melodies to the Huguenot Psalter, the psalm-tunes of which famous work are largely based upon folk-tunes and popular French tunes of the day. These secular tunes, however, were seldom adopted by the French Reformed Church in their entirety. Calvin, in a preface written in 1543, says that they have been " moderées," in order that they may have " le poids et majesté," proper to sacred music. It is true that the melody of the 138th Psalm differs only in a few notes from that of the chanson " Une pastourelle gentille," as it appears in Attaignant's collection of songs published about 1530. But in most cases the psalm-tunes can only be said to be based on secular tunes, in that they contain isolated lines or special characteristic features of the latter. It was this use of certain phrases from the chanson " Petite camusette " which drew a laugh from the austere Calvin—" his only one," as Schweitzer adds. Two of the best-known chorale melodies borrowed from the French psalter are " Freu' dich sehr o meine Seele," and " Wenn wir in höchsten Nöthen sein." The former, in the opinion of Winterfeld and Döring,[1] belonged originally to a hunting-song. This view is supported by the general character of the melody, which in places somewhat suggests the call of the huntsman's horn. Moreover, it is set in the French psalter to the 42nd Psalm, and we are told by the chronicler Florimond de Rémond that the Dauphin, who in 1547 became Henry II. of France, sang this psalm " à la chasse." There is, however, no evidence to show that the melody in question

[1] See his " Choral-kunde," p. 55.

was the actual one sung "at the hunt": it is even doubtful whether it was set to the psalm before 1547. The melody " Wenn wir in höchsten Nöthen sein," which in the French psalter is set to the hymn of the Commandments and the 140th Psalm, is also probably of secular origin.

We see how wide a use the Evangelical Church made of secular melodies. Some of these the Reformers borrowed from contemporary art; others are genuine folk-tunes. If we compare the general character of these melodies with that of the melodies of the old German folk-hymns, we notice certain points of difference. The secular melodies on the whole wear a more modern aspect. This we should naturally expect of some of them, for they are of a comparatively late date. That it is true also of those derived from ancient folk-song is largely due to the fact that, by belonging, as it were, to the individual, not to the congregation, they were far more subject to variation, this being naturally mainly in the direction of modern idiom. The secular melodies show signs of emancipation from the old tonal system. In them the Ionian mode transposed to F (the key of F major) predominates, and, of the other modes, those that approximate to the minor key, namely, the Æolian and Dorian, are by far the most common. Another distinguishing characteristic is their strongly marked and varied rhythm. The difference, however, between these two classes of melodies is far less than that which to-day marks the secular from the sacred type. During the early centuries of the art's development the Church was the only school of music, and thus even the secular tunes bear to some extent the mark of the cloister. There is a nobility about them even though, as is often the case, the words may be commonplace and frivolous. They seem to have a certain aloofness from their text, expressing, indeed, its general sentiment, whether of joy or sorrow, but raising this sentiment to a higher moral plane. And it is for this reason that they have proved so well fitted for the service of the church; that they have lived in the chorale books, as in their natural home. We cannot but feel that Hassler's beautiful melody has much more in common with Gerhardt's hymn of Divine love than with the little song of human love from which it was taken. And so it is with most of them; it is not until they have been set to a sacred text that they really come to their own and reveal their full beauty.

IV.—MELODIES EXPRESSLY COMPOSED FOR THE EVANGELICAL SERVICE

Most of the melodies of this group belong to the seventeenth century —to that great creative period of the chorale adorned by the names of Nicolai, Herberger, Rinkart, Franck and Gerhardt, poets, and Johann Crüger, prince of Lutheran melodists. The number of original melodies written during the early years of the Reformation is comparatively small. It was natural that the Evangelical Church should first make use of the old tunes ready to hand. There could be no question as to their suitability: they had stood the test of ages and were in many cases already well known. Moreover, Luther saw that the new song should be built up on the foundation of the old. Composers had yet to learn the true principles of the congregational hymn-tune, and these had first to be illustrated in examples selected or composed by Luther himself and a small circle of his musical friends. Again, the spiritual seeds of the Reformation required time to grow; the widespread religious fervour, which later became the mainspring of German music and poetry and so brought both arts into the service of the church, had yet to be kindled.

There are, however, among the new melodies of the early chorale books some of the finest in Lutheran hymnody. "Ein' feste Burg" appeared in 1529, "Vom Himmel hoch" and "Allein Gott in der Hoh' sei Ehr'" in 1539, and "O Lamm Gottes unschuldig" (in its first form) in 1542. But it is to Walther, not to Luther or Decius, that we must assign the largest share of the new melodies belonging to the first half of the century. He lived, indeed, till 1570, but it is probable that he wrote little after 1551, when he brought out his last edition of the "Gesangbüchlein." It may be said generally of the melodies attributed to him, that the earlier ones are finer than the later; that most of the earlier have survived and most of the later before long fell out of use. Among the important new melodies of this period we must also include Greiter's "Es sind doch selig alle die" and Dachstein's "An Wasserflüssen Babylon."

In the second half of the sixteenth century the number of original melodies began rapidly to increase. Like those of Luther and Decius, many of them are the work of the poet himself. It is surprising how often, especially in the early history of the chorale, we find poetic and musical gifts of a high order combined in the same person. It is probable that Selnecker wrote over forty melodies for his own hymns, and Hermann, one of the most gifted melodists of this period, is also the author of the two fine hymns " Lobt Gott ihr Christen alle gleich " and " Erschienen ist der herrlich Tag," as well as much secular verse. Many also of the new melodies were composed by church cantors for the hymns of their pastors. Hermann set to music not only his own texts but those of Matthesius, and von Burck many of Helmbold's. The outstanding names belonging to the years 1550–1590 are those of Waldis, Hermann, von Burck, Selnecker, and Steurlein.

The richest period of German hymnody was a time of great national distress. The frequent outbreaks of the plague at the end of the sixteenth century and in the early years of the seventeenth, and the prolonged barbarism of the Thirty Years War, reduced the country to the last stage of exhaustion and misery. Amid this wreckage of earthly happiness the thoughts of all spiritually-minded men turned fervently to religion and it was in sacred song that their deep feelings of piety found expression. " Germany," says Schweitzer, " in its bitterest need created a religious poetry to which nothing in the world can compare and before which even the splendour of the Psalter pales." These hymns are in many cases a mirror of contemporary events. While the plague was raging at Frauenstadt in 1613 Herberger wrote " Valet will ich dir geben," in which " the devout soul bids farewell to the world "; Rinkart's " Nun danket alle Gott " gave voice to the nation's gratitude for the conclusion of peace in 1648. To the call of the hymn-writers musicians were not slow to respond. Of the countless melodies written for the church at this time, many, of course, were not destined to live, but to most of the Evangelical musicians of this period there remains at least one to keep his name in remembrance. The melodies of Johann Crüger, about twenty of which are still in use, are the crown and climax of this great creative impulse. For profusion and sustained excellence, his work in this form is unequalled in the whole history of hymnody. In the chorale books of to-day we find some three or four of Johann Schop's and Rudolph Ahle's melodies, a smaller number belonging to each of the distinguished choral composers, Eccard, Calvisius, Vulpius, Gesius and Prätorius, and two attributed to Nicolai; while the names of Teschner, Neumark, Heinrich Albert,[1] Melchior Franck[2] and Gastorius occur in connection with one melody only.

The question of Luther's and Walther's place in the history of the chorale has already been discussed: it remains to sketch very briefly, in the following summaries, the life and work of the other important writers of hymn-tunes.

1. Matthäus Greiter was a monk and singer of Strassburg Cathedral. In 1524 he left the cloister and married, and a few years later he became Assistant Pastor of St. Martin's Church in Strassburg. In 1549 he conformed to the "Interim"[3] and founded a choir-school in connection with the Interim services of the Cathedral. He died in 1552. Greiter is probably the composer of the melody "O Mensch bewein' dein' Sünde gross'," which first appeared in the "Deutsch Kirchenamt" of 1525, set to his hymn "Es sind doch selig alle die."

2. Wolfgang Dachstein was a monk and Organist of Strassburg Cathedral till 1524, when, like Greiter, he became a Protestant. In 1525 he was Organist and Assistant Pastor of St. Thomas' Church in Strassburg. Nothing is known of his later life. It is assumed that he himself wrote the beautiful melody belonging to his hymn "An Wasserflüssen Babylon."

3. Nikolaus Decius (von Hofe or Hovesch) was born probably at Hof in Upper Franconia. In 1519 he was Provost of the Convent at Steterburg, near Wolfenbüttel. One of the earliest of the Reformers, he resigned this office in 1522 and was appointed master in the St. Katharine and Egidien School at Brunswick. In 1523 he was instituted Preacher in the Church of St. Nicolas at Stettin. He died at Stettin in 1541. We are told in Rethmeyer's "Kirchenhistorie" of 1710 that Decius was an excellent musician and himself composed the melodies of his hymns.

---

[1] Composer of the well-known melody "Gott des Himmels und der Erde."

[2] Probably the composer of the melody "Jerusalem, du hochgebaute Stadt."

[3] The term was applied to certain edicts and decrees passed by the Emperor and the Diets during the Reformation in Germany, with the object of temporarily settling religious controversy. Thus, an "Interim" established a temporary *modus vivendi* between Catholics and Protestants.

4. Nikolaus Hermann (1485 ?-1561) was for many years Cantor at Joachimsthal in Bohemia, working in close friendship with his pastor, Matthesius. He was not a polyphonist, for his music is never written in more than two parts, but he composed simple and popular melodies for his own hymns and songs and those of Matthesius. He had a very modest opinion of his own work, which was intended only for " children and the home." He says of his hymns: " If anyone thinks so highly of them as to have them sung in church, he does so on his own responsibility." Hermann made great use of his melodies, often setting the same one both to secular and sacred words. Most of his hymns and songs appeared separately but were afterwards collected in " Die Sontags-evangelia " of 1560 and " Die Historien von der Sindflut " published in 1562. Matthesius wrote a preface to the latter, in which he speaks of " his old and dear friend, musician and poet, whose songs are adorned with lovely melodies."

5. Nikolaus Selnecker (1528-1592) was a man of many gifts and restless energy. A voluminous writer of prose and sacred verse, a polyphonist and composer of melodies, he was Organist of the Castle Chapel at Nürnberg at the age of twelve, Court Preacher at Dresden in 1557, afterwards Professor at Jena and Leipzig, and in many other spheres of activity. His life was chequered by many vicissitudes, due to opposition aroused by his strong religious opinions and controversial nature. In his " Geistliche Psalmen, Lieder und Kirchengesänge " of 1587 there are over forty melodies which, presumably, he himself composed.

6. Joachim von Burck (1541 ?-1610) was Organist and Cantor of the Church of St. Blasius[1] at Mühlhausen in Thuringia, and, as such, a predecessor of J. S. Bach. As a polyphonist his style is simple and tuneful, modelled, as he himself tells us, on that of the Italian Villanella. Most of his melodies, which are of a light, popular character, were

---

[1] The church, which dates from the fourteenth century, is a fine, impressive building, with handsome outside buttresses surmounted by pinnacles and two beautiful western spires. The organ in 1912, when the present writer played it, was much out of repair. It was blown by means of four broad, projecting levers, with a drop of about six feet, and worked, by the weight of the body, by two blowers. Each blower worked two levers, mounting by a ladder and descending upon each lever in turn.

composed for the "Christian Rhymes" (German and Latin) of his pastor Ludwig Helmbold.

7. Johann Steurlein (1546-1613) held the office of Public Notary at Wasungen, a small town in Thuringia. He was a musician of considerable ability, the style of his choral writing being very similar to that of von Burck. He published several collections of sacred songs and is remembered to-day by his melody "Das alte Jahr vergangen ist."

8. Johann Eccard was born at Mühlhausen in 1553, and was first a pupil of von Burck and afterwards of Orlando Lasso in Munich. In 1578 he was "Musikus" in the service of Count Fugger at Augsburg, and in 1608 Kapellmeister at the Berlin Court. He died in 1611. One of the finest polyphonists of his time, he is important for his excellent settings of the chorale melodies, rather than for the melodies which he himself composed.

9. Bartholomäus Gesius (c. 1555-1613 or 1614) was first a student of theology but afterwards devoted himself to music. In 1593 he became Cantor at Frankfurt-on-the-Oder, where he remained till his death. He brought out several collections of four and five part settings of the chorale melodies. Among the melodies set are a few which presumably he wrote himself, the most important of these being "Heut triumphiret Gottes Sohn."

10. Seth Calvisius (or Kalwitz) was born at Gorsleben in 1556. In 1572 he was a "Kurrend-Schuler" (a poor schoolboy who sang in the streets for his livelihood) at Magdeburg, as Luther had been at Eisenach. He studied at the Universities of Helmstedt and Leipzig. In 1594 he became Cantor of St. Thomas' Church and a master in St. Thomas' School at Leipzig, where he remained till his death in 1615. He made many excellent four-part arrangements of the chorale melodies (his "Harmonia Cantionum Ecclesiasticarum" of 1597 contains one hundred and twenty-seven), but only a few of the melodies themselves were composed by him. His most important melody is "In dich hab' ich gehoffet Herr," which appeared first in 1581, and again in his "Hymni Sacri Latini et Germanici" of 1594. It occurs several times in Bach's works.[1]

11. Philipp Nicolai (1556-1608) was born at Mengeringhausen in

[1] See Bach's "St. Matthew Passion," No. 38.

Waldeck, where his father was Pastor. He studied theology at Erfurt and Wittenburg. From 1596 to 1601 he was Pastor at Unna in Westphalia, his ministrations, especially during the plague which broke out there in 1597, being marked by the utmost devotion. In 1601 he became Chief Pastor of St. Catharine's Church at Hamburg. His " Freuden Spiegel des ewigen Lebens "—a religious treatise, with a supplement of four hymns—was published in 1598. Three of these hymns, namely, " Wie Schön leuchtet der Morgenstern," " Wachet auf," and " So wünsch' ich nun ein' gute Nacht der Welt und lass' sie fahren," were written by himself, and one, " Herr Christ, thu' mir verleihen," by his brother Jeremias. The melodies of the first two hymns are noted, and are in all probability the work of Philipp Nicolai himself : those of the other two are indicated by name only.

12. Melchior Vulpius was born at Wasungen about the year 1560. He was Cantor at Weimar in 1600, and died there in 1616. His hymn-books of 1604 and 1609 contain three, four, and five part settings of the chorale melodies, among which are several new melodies of his own. Two of the latter are " Christus der ist mein Leben,"[1] and " Jesu Kreuz, Leiden und Pein," both of which occur in Bach's works and are still in common use.

13. Hans Leo Hassler[2] (1564-1612) was born at Nürnberg. After studying for some years under Andrea Gabrieli in Venice, he entered the service of Count Fugger at Augsburg as Organist. He returned to Nürnberg, and in 1601 was Organist of the Frauenkirche. In 1608 he was appointed " Musikus " and " Kammer-organist " at the Dresden Court. Hassler wrote a large amount both of sacred and secular music and was undoubtedly one of the most distinguished musicians of his time. Zahn calls him " the greatest composer of the classical period of church music." Proske, in his collection of ancient church music entitled " Musica Divina " which was published at Ratisbon in

---

[1] See " Hymns Ancient and Modern," No. 405.

[2] This biographical sketch is inserted here for the sake of convenience. Hassler wrote many settings of the chorale melodies, which are of the very highest excellence, but the famous melody by which his name lives to-day in the hymn-books is of secular origin, and therefore belongs properly to Group III. of the classification.

1853-1861, says of his style that " it unites all the greatest beauty and dignity that can be found in both the Italian and German art of that day." Hassler's melody, " Mein G'müt ist mir verwirret,"[1] which was soon "raised to a higher sphere" by being set to the hymns " Herzlich thut mich verlangen " and "O Haupt voll Blut und Wunden," is first found in a collection of secular songs (" Lustgarten neuer deutscher Gesänge ") brought out in 1601.

14. Michael Prätorius (1571-1621) was Kapellmeister in 1596 to the Duke of Brunswick, and in 1613 to the Elector of Saxony. He was an indefatigable composer of church music : his chief work, the " Musæ Sioniæ," contains no less than twelve hundred and forty-four settings of the chorale melodies. Some of these settings are in the form of motets, others are simple in character, suitable for congregational use. Only a few of the melodies are new and these are of no great importance.

15. Melchior Teschner, in the early years of the seventeenth century, was Cantor of the Church " zum Kripplein Christi " at Frauenstadt in Silesia. He composed two musical settings of the hymn " Valet will ich dir geben," written by his pastor, Herberger. The melody of the first of these is still in common use and known in England as " St. Theodulph."[2] Teschner in his latter years, as we learn from his signature to a Latin epicedium on Herberger, written in 1627, became a pastor at Frauenstadt.

16. Johann Schop was born at the end of the sixteenth century, probably at Hamburg. He was a talented player both on the organ and violin, and, after a career at Wolfenbüttel and the Danish Court, became in 1621 Musical Director to the Town Council and Kapellmeister at Hamburg. His best-known melodies were written for the hymns of his friend Johann Rist, pastor at Wedel, near Hamburg.

17. Johann Crüger (1598–1662) was born at Gross-Breesen, in Prussia, and educated chiefly at the Jesuit College of Olmütz, at the School of Poetry at Ratisbon, and the University of Wittenberg. In 1622 he was appointed Cantor of St. Nicholas' Church in Berlin,

---

[1] The text is a love-song of five verses, the initial letters of which spell the name " Maria."

[2] See " Hymns Ancient and Modern," No. 98.

where he remained till his death. In his own time Crüger had great reputation both as an author and composer; he wrote several books on the theory of music and composed a great number of concerti and large choral works. To-day, however, his fame rests on his splendid hymn-tunes. In this golden treasury, from the deeply penitential "Herzliebster Jesu, was hast du verbrochen" to the triumphant "Nun danket alle Gott," many phases of devotional feeling find expression. Perhaps, however, what is most characteristic of Crüger's work is the beautiful serenity of such melodies as "Schmücke dich, o liebe Seele," "Jesu, meine Freude," "O wie selig seid ihr doch, ihr Frommen," and "Jesu, meine Zuversicht."

18. Georg Neumark was born in 1621 at Langensalza, a small town in Thuringia, and was educated at a school in Gotha and at Königsberg University. In 1641 he took the post of private tutor in a family at Kiel. Here it was, as he himself tells us, that he wrote the words of his well-known hymn, "Wer nur den lieben Gott lässt walten." In 1651 he became Chancery Registrar and Librarian at Weimar, where he died in 1681. He published two collections of sacred and secular songs, namely, the "Lustwäldchen" of 1652 and the "Fortgepflanzter Lustwald"[1] of 1657. It is in the latter that we first find his famous melody for the above-mentioned hymn.

19. Rudolph Ahle (1625–1673) was born at Mühlhausen, in Thuringia. In 1646 he was Cantor of St. Andrew's Church at Erfurt. Returning to his native town, he became Organist[2] of the Church of St. Blasius in 1649, member of the Town Council in 1655, and Burgomaster in 1661. He composed a great many melodies of a simple aria type for hymns written by the Mühlhausen clergy and himself.

20. Severus Gastorius was Cantor at Jena about 1675. Beyond this fact we know nothing of his life except what we learn in a story about his well-known melody "Was Gott thut, das ist wohlgethan." We are told that a friend of his, named Rodigast, wrote the hymn to console Gastorius during an illness, and that, having recovered, Gastorius set it to music as a thank-offering. The story adds that the hymn was sung every week at the composer's house by his choir.

---

[1] See note on the melody "Wer nur den lieben Gott lässt walten," in Part II.

[2] His son, who succeeded him, was J. S. Bach's immediate predecessor.

PART II
THE MELODIES WITH HISTORICAL NOTES

REMARKS ON THE NOTATION OF THE MELODIES

1. The melodies have been copied by the present writer from Zahn's "Die Melodien," from Wolfrum's "Die Entstehung und erste Entwickelung des deutschen Kirchenliedes," and from original sources—namely, the "Erfurt Enchiridion" and Walther's "Gesanbüchlein" (in modern reprints), and the "Praxis pietatis melica" (the copy of the 1656 edition in the British Museum). In Zahn's "Die Melodien" the melodies appear in shorter notes than those of the original notation, minims being used for semibreves, crotchets for minims, and quavers for crotchets. They are given in the earliest form found in the post-Reformation hymn-books, which form, however, in the case of the pre-Reformation melodies and the later melodies of secular origin, is not always the earliest extant.

2. It will be noticed that in many cases an accidental is placed over the note. Such accidentals do not occur in the original, and must be regarded as suggestions. The ancient use in polyphonic music was to leave the accidental sharpening or flattening of notes to the discretion of the singers, who, being well versed in the rules of solmization, thoroughly understood where such should take place.

3. With regard to the frequently used time-signatures C and ₵, it may be said that, in the older melodies, they indicate a measuring of the melody into portions of four or two unit notes, but not necessarily a system of accentuation.

4. In their original notation the melodies of the sixteenth century are almost invariably written in the C clef. The G clef is used here for convenience.

(1) CHRIST IST ERSTANDEN.[1] *(From Klug's Gesangbuch of* 1535.)

---

[1] For translation see p. 75.

This Easter hymn, which originally consisted of but one verse and Hallelujas, is probably the oldest German sacred folk-song in present use. There is evidence to show that in the thirteenth century it was well known, and, in some churches, even incorporated in the liturgical service. It is frequently mentioned in manuscripts of the fifteenth century, and the beginning of the hymn is found in most of the Latin Office-books which were printed in Germany between 1480 and 1522. It was sung usually in connection with the Sequence "Victimæ Paschali," and sometimes just before or after the sermon. The melody, which is undoubtedly coeval with the text, is first found in a Munich manuscript of the fifteenth century. It has appeared in many forms, the above later version, like that of the text, being an extension of the original.

(2) NUN BITTEN WIR DEN HEILIGEN GEIST. (*From Walther's "Gesang-büchlein" of* 1524.)

This old Whitsuntide hymn, like "Christ ist erstanden," had originally only one verse. It is mentioned in a thirteenth-century manuscript of a sermon preached by Brother Berthold of Ratisbon (see Part I., p. 34), and again, in 1340, in connection with two

Miracle Plays. The melody, which is undoubtedly the old original one, was first printed in Walther's "Gesangbüchlein" of 1524, where, besides the original text, are also Luther's three new verses. Wizel, in his " Psaltes Ecclesiasticus " of 1550, prints the hymn with the remark, " Here sing the whole congregation."

(3) DIES SIND DIE HEILGEN ZEHN GEBOT.   (*From the "Erfurt Enchiri-*
      (*Dorian Version.*)   *dion" of 1524 : original notation.*)

(*Luther.*)[1]

We have here, as we are expressly told in the " Erfurt Enchiridion," the melody of the Pilgrims' hymn " In Gottes Namen fahren wir," which is mentioned about 1215 in a poem by Gottfried of Strassburg. It is remarkable that the melody, as it is found in the earlier chorale books, sometimes has, and at other times has not, the signature of B♭. In the latter case the note B is accidentally flattened in the last line on " Sinai." Thus there are two readings : the one in the Dorian mode (transposed), the other in the Mixolydian mode with a Dorian ending. Winterfeld and Böhme point out that in the thirteenth century the use of leading-notes was becoming recognized, and pronounce the latter reading to be the original melody. In the seventeenth century the Dorian version fell permanently out of use.

[1] Here, and in similar cases, the name given in brackets is that of the author of the text.

(4) ES IST DAS HEIL UNS KOMMEN HER.

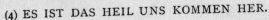

(From "Etlich Christlich Lider" of 1524, the so-called "Achtliederbuch.")

Es ist das Heil uns kom-men her   von Gnad und lau-ter
Die Werk die hel-fen nim-mer-mehr, sie mö-gen nicht be-

Gü - te ;   Der Glaub sieht Je-sum Christ-um an,   der hat gnug
hü - ten.

für uns all ge-than ;   er ist der Mitt-ler wor - den.

(Paul Speratus.)

This beautiful Mixolydian melody occurs both in the "Achtliederbuch" and the "Erfurt Enchiridion." In the former it is utilized for four hymns and in the latter for two—namely, Paul Speratus' "Es ist das Heil uns kommen her," and Luther's "Nun freut euch liebe Christen g'mein." It originally belonged to the pre-Reformation hymn "Freu' dich du werthe Christenheit," with which it is first found in a late fifteenth-century Processionale of the Miltenberg Monastery. (See Baümker's "Das katholische deutsche Kirchenlied," Vol. I., p. 545.)

(5) KOMM GOTT SCHÖPFER HEILIGER GEIST.

(From Babst's Gesangbüch of 1545.)

Komm Gott Schöp - fer, hei - li ger   Geist,   be - such

das Herz der Men-schen dein,   mit Gna - den sie füll,

wie du   weisst,   dass dein Ge - schöpf vor - hin sein.

(Luther.)

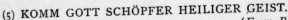

The text is Luther's translation of the Latin hymn " Veni Creator Spiritus " (see Part I., p. 37); the melody is a simplified popular version of the original plainsong melody of the Latin hymn. The Lutheran version of the old melody has several forms. The earliest of these, with Luther's text, occurs in the " Erfurt Enchiridion "; Klug and Babst have a better form (as above) which is still in use.

(6) CHRISTUS DER UNS SELIG MACHT. (*From Wolff's Gesangbuch of 1570.*)

Chri - stus der uns se - lig macht, kein Bös hat began - gen, der ward für uns in der Nacht als ein
Dieb ge - fan - gen, Ge - führt vor gott - lo - se
Leut und fälsch - lich ver - kla - get, ver - lacht, ver - höhnt
und ver - speit wie denn die Schrift sa - - get.

(*Weisse.*)

Text and melody are first found in " Ein new Gesengbuchlen "—a hymn-book brought out by Michael Weisse in 1531 for the German members of the community of the Bohemian Brethren—and were later incorporated in the Lutheran hymn-books. The text is Weisse's German version of the hymn of the Hours, " Patris sapientia," which is found in manuscripts of the fourteenth century. The melody no doubt originated with the Latin text.

(7) O WELT ICH MUSS DICH LASSEN.

(Melody and secular text from the 1549 *edition of Forster's Liederbuch, first published in* 1539.)

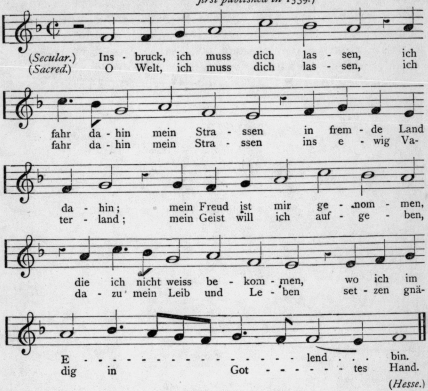

(*Secular.*) Ins - bruck, ich muss dich las - sen, ich
(*Sacred.*) O Welt, ich muss dich las - sen, ich

fahr da - hin mein Stra - ssen in frem - de Land
fahr da - hin mein Stra - ssen ins e - wig Va-

da - hin; mein Freud ist mir ge - nom - men,
ter - land; mein Geist will ich auf - ge - ben,

die ich nicht weiss be - kom - men, wo ich im
da - zu mein Leib und Le - ben set - zen gnä-

E - - - - - - - - - - - - - lend . . . bin.
dig in Got - - - - - tes Hand.

(*Hesse.*)

The four-part musical setting of the secular text, of which this melody is the soprano part, was written by Heinrich Isaak about the year 1475. The origin of the melody has been disputed. According to Böhme, it probably comes from folk-song. Kade, on the other hand, has maintained that if Isaak had been making a contrapuntal setting of a melody, he would have given it, according to the prevailing custom, to the tenor voice. In a paper published in 1873 he stated his opinion that the tenor part of Isaak's music is the old and principal melody, and that the melody in question is one of the added parts. Böhme, however, declared that this view could not be accepted until the tenor part could be traced back and shown to have had an independent origin. The above melody is first found allied to a sacred text in 1505. In a Munich codex of that date mention is made of "a little song to SS. Anna and Joachim, to the tune 'Insbruck ich muss dich lassen.'" In 1555 it appeared, in a separate print, set to Hesse's "O Welt ich muss dich lassen." Gerhardt's Evening hymn, "Nun ruhen alle Wälder," with which it afterwards became associated, was written about the year 1663.

(8) VATER UNSER IM HIMMELREICH. (*From Schumann's Gesangbuch of 1539.*)

Vat - er un - ser im Him - mel - reich, der du uns
al - le hei - ssest gleich Brü - der sein und dich ru - fen an
und willst das Be - ten von uns han, gieb, dass nicht bet al -
lein der Mund, hilf, dass es geh von Her - zen Grund.

(*Luther.*)

Luther, as soon as he had finished his text, set himself to compose a melody for it. The melody, however, did not satisfy him, for there is still extant his crossed-out sketch of it (see Part I., p. 22). The text and the above Dorian melody occur in the "Luther Codex" of 1530—a recently discovered manuscript part-book which Walther gave to Luther in 1530, containing the tenor part of a collection of polyphonic works. This does not, however, prove that the hymn was written at this early date, for it is probable that additions were made to the "Luther Codex" later. Indeed, it can hardly have been written before 1535, as it does not appear in Klug's Gesangbuch of that year, which was brought out under Luther's direction. The first hymn-book to have it is Schumann's of 1539. The origin of this famous melody has been much disputed. Both Böhme and Baümker, however, are of the opinion that it comes from folk-song. They point out (1) that the melody in the 1544 edition of Walther's "Gesangbüchlein" has the superscription "auf Berckreien Weise" (the probable translation being "after the manner of an alpine song"), which, though its meaning is obscure, seems to point to a secular origin ; (2) that the melody is found later set "to all possible texts"; (3) that before the middle of the century there appeared a version of it, written in triple time, and decidedly secular in character.

(9) DURCH ADAMS FALL IST GANZ VERDERBT. (*From Klug's Gesangbuch of 1535.*)

Durch A - dams Fall ist ganz ver - derbt men - schlich Na-
Das - selb Gift ist auf uns ge - erbt, dass wir nicht

tur und We - sen ; ohn Got - tes Trost, der uns er - löst
konn - ten g'ne - sen,

hat von dem gros - sen Scha - den, da - rein die

Schlang E - vam be - zwang, Gotts Zorn auf sich zu la - den.

(*Spengler.*)

The melody appeared in Klug's Gesangbuch of 1535, superseding two others which Walther had set to the hymn in 1524. Its origin was uncertain until Böhme discovered a separate print (made about 1530) of two hymns, the second of which—namely, the above chorale—has the title "Ein Lyed, von Adams fal In einem newen thon, den man singet von der schlacht vor Pavia." We have, therefore, in the above melody the so-called "Pavier-ton," often mentioned during the sixteenth century. It belonged to a song about the Battle of Pavia which took place in 1525.

(10) HERZLICH THUT MICH VERLANGEN.

(From the Görlitz "Harmoniæ Sacræ" of 1613.)

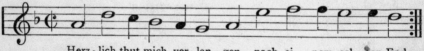

Herz - lich thut mich ver - lan - gen nach ei - nem sel - gen End,
Weil ich hie bin um - fan - gen mit Trüb - sal und E - lend.

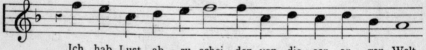

Ich hab Lust ab - zu - schei - den von die - ser ar - gen Welt,

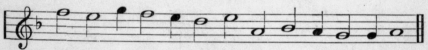

sehn mich nach ew - ger Freu - den; O Je - su, komm nur bald!

(Knoll.)

The melody was composed by Hans Leo Hassler. In 1601 he brought out his "Lustgarten neuer deutscher Gesänge, Balletti, Galliarden und Intraden mit vier, fünf und acht Stimmen" (Pleasure-garden of new German songs, balletti, galliards and intrades for four, five, and eight voices). Here, as the soprano part of a five-part musical setting of the love-song "Mein G'müt ist mir verwirret, das macht ein' Jungfrau zart'" (My heart is distracted by a tender maiden), the melody is first found. In 1613 the whole five-part setting was printed in the song-book of a school at Görlitz, entitled "Harmoniæ Sacræ," where, however, for the original text is substituted Christoph Knoll's Funeral hymn, "Herzlich thut mich verlangen." It was probably Buchwalder, Cantor at Görlitz, who made the adaptation. The melody is also associated with Gerhardt's Passion hymn, "O Haupt voll Blut und Wunden," written about 1656.

(11) AUS TIEFER NOT SCHREI ICH ZU DIR.

(*From Walther's "Gesangbüchlein" of* 1524.)

Aus tie - fer Not schrei ich zu dir, Herr
Dein gnä - dig Oh - ren kehr zu mir, und

Gott, er - hör mein Ru - - fen, denn so du wilt
mei - ner Bitt sie öf - - fen;

das se - - hen an, wie man - che Sünd ich hab . . .

ge - than, wer kann, Herr, für dir blei - - - ben.

(*Luther.*)

Luther's text occurs in all the three hymn-books of the year 1524—namely, the "Achtliederbuch," the "Erfurt Enchiridion," and Walther's "Gesangbüchlein." The fine Phrygian melody occurs in the last two of these. The "Erfurt Enchiridion" has it in unison, Walther's "Gesangbüchlein" in a four-part setting. The melody, which was probably composed by Walther, has played an important part in organ music from the time of Bach to the present day.

(12) MIT FRIED UND FREUD ICH FAHR DAHIN.

(From Walther's "Gesangbüchlein" of 1524.)

Mit Fried und Freud ich fahr da - hin in ....
Got - - - tes .. Wil - le ; ge - trost ist mir
mein Herz ... und Sinn, sanft und stil - - - -
le. Wie ... Gott mir ver - hei - ssen ...
hat ; der Tod ist mein Schlaf wor - - - - den.

(Luther.)

This beautiful melody is first found in Walther's " Gesangbüchlein "
of 1524, set polyphonically for four voices. From the fact that it does
not also occur in the " Erfurt Enchiridion " we may attribute it to
Walther more readily than No. 11 (see Part I., p. 25). Moreover, its
melismatic character suggests that it originated as part of the polyphony. The melody later assumed a somewhat simpler form.

(13) NUN FREUT EUCH LIEBEN CHRISTEN G'MEIN.

(From "Etlich Christlich Lider" of 1524.)

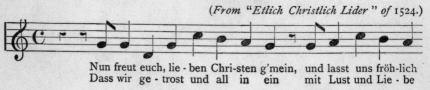

Nun freut euch, lie - ben Chri - sten g'mein, und lasst uns fröh - lich
Dass wir ge - trost und all in ein   mit Lust und Lie - be

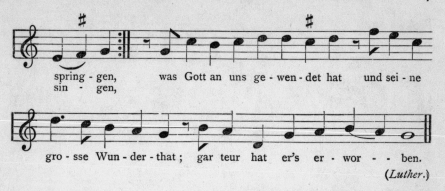

spring - gen,   was Gott an uns ge - wen - det hat   und sei - ne
sin - gen,

gro - sse Wun - der - that ;   gar teur hat er's er - wor - - ben.

(*Luther.*)

The melody is one of the four which occur in the so-called "Achtliederbuch" ("Etlich Christlich Lider" of 1524). Walther's "Gesangbüchlein" has it in an elaborate form. It does not occur in the "Erfurt Enchiridion," which book, though it gives the text, assigns it to another melody—namely, "Es ist das Heil." Zahn assumes that the above melody was composed by Luther or Walther. It may be that Walther's form of it is the original melody, and that this was simplified for the "Achtliederbuch."

(14) O MENSCH, BEWEIN DEIN SÜNDE GROSS.

(*Melody from the Strassburg "Psalmen" of* 1526.)

O Mensch, be - wein dein Sün - de gross ; da - rum Chri - stus sein's Va-
Von ei - ner Jung-frau rein und zart   für uns er hie ge - bo-

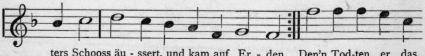

ters Schooss äu - ssert, und kam auf Er - den. Den'n Tod-ten er das
ren ward, er   wollt der Mitt-ler wer - den.

Le - ben gab,   und legt da - bei all Krank-heit ab,   bis sich die

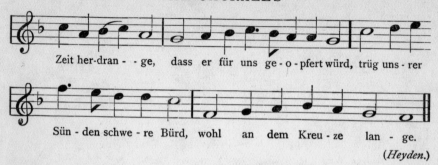

Zeit her-dran - - ge, dass er für uns ge - o - pfert würd, trüg uns - rer

Sün - den schwe - re Bürd, wohl an dem Kreu - ze lan - ge.

(Heyden.)

The melody was most probably composed by Matthäus Greiter. In Part III. of the "Deutsch Kirchenamt" of 1525, where it first appeared, and in the "Psalmen, Gebett, and Kirchenübung," published at Strassburg in 1526, it was set to Greiter's hymn "Es sind doch selig alle die" (see Part I., p. 10). In Calvin's Psalter of 1539 it was adapted to a version of Psalm XXXVI., "En moy le secret pensement." It became associated (as above) with Heyden's hymn about 1584. The tune was brought into English use in the "Four Score and Seven Psalmes" of 1561, where it was set to Psalm CXIII.

(15) EIN FESTE BURG IST UNSER GOTT.

(From Klug's Gesangbuch of 1535.)

Ein fe - ste Burg ist un - - ser
Er hilft uns frei aus al - - ler

Gott, ein gu - te Wehr und Waf - - - - - fen;
Not, die uns jetzt hat be - trof - - - - - fen.

Der alt...... bö - - - se Feind mit Ernst ers jetzt meint,

gross Macht und viel List sein grau - sam Rü - stung

ist ;   auf Erd ist nicht seins Glei - - - - - chen.

(*Luther.*)

The controversy about the origin of this famous melody has been of
a somewhat partisan character.   Catholic hymnologists, for the most
part, maintain that the melody is derived from plainsong.   Baümker,
the most definite of these, states that it is constructed line by line out
of certain phrases (which he quotes) taken from the Roman Gradual—
namely, from the Credos of the " Missa de Angelis," the " Missa in
dupplicibus," and the " Missa in dupplicibus solemnioribus."   Zahn, on
the Protestant side, says that by searching through the Roman
Gradual, and choosing a phrase here and there, one could find equally
good reasons for assigning every old melody to a Gregorian source.
The truth lies between these extreme views.   Köstlin points out that
the plainsong phrases quoted by Baümker differ in important respects
from those of the hymn-tune, but at the same time he is in general
agreement with Schweitzer, who says that the melody is "woven
out of Gregorian reminiscences."   Text and melody appeared in the
lost Klug's Gesangbuch of 1529, the contents of which, however, were
reprinted in the " Journal von und für Deutschland " in the year 1788.
The earliest extant copy of the text occurs in an Augsburg hymn-
book of 1529 ; that of the melody (if we disregard its occurrence in the
" Luther Codex " [see No. 8], which, though dated 1530, probably
contains some tunes added later) in Gutknecht's " Kirchengesänge,"
published at Nürnberg in 1531.   Böhme and Wackernagel found the
melody also in a copy (the only remaining one) of Rauscher's " Geistliche Lieder " of 1531 (the second edition of Klug's Gesangbuch of
1529).   Zahn, however, says that this copy, which used to be in the
Library at Helmstedt, has since disappeared.

(16) VOM HIMMEL HOCH DA KOMM ICH HER.

(From Schumann's Gesangbuch of 1539.)

Vom Him - mel hoch da komm ich her; ich
bring euch gu - te neu - e Mär; der gu - ten Mär bring
ich so viel, da - von ich sing'n und sa - - gen will.

(Luther.)

The text is Luther's "sacred parody" of the folk-song "Aus fremdem Landen komm' ich her." He originally set it to the tune of the folk-song, but this he afterwards rejected on account of its secular associations. The hymn was first set to the above fine melody, which is probably Luther's own (see Part I. p. 23), in Schumann's Gesangbuch of 1539.

(17) ALLEIN GOTT IN DER HÖH SEI EHR. *(From Schumann's Gesangbuch of* 1539.)

Al - lein Gott in der Höhe sei Ehr und
Da - rum dass nun und nim - mer-mehr uns

Dank für sei - ne Gna - - de, Ein Wohl-
rüh - ren kann kein Scha - - de;

ge - fallen Gott an uns hat ; nun ist gross Fried ohn

Un - ter - lass, all Feh - de hat nun ein En - - de.

(Decius.)

Both the hymn, which is a free translation of the "Gloria in excelsis," and the melody, which is partly based on passages from an old Easter Gloria, were written by Nikolaus Decius. The hymn in low-German, beginning "Alleyne Godt," is first found in a hymn-book of 1526, but without melody. The above melody and high-German text are first found in Schumann's Gesangbuch of 1539, the editor of which must have had before him a copy of the earlier text with the melody, as he has retained for "allein" the three notes used for the low-German "alleyne." It is remarkable that this hymn does not occur in any hymn-book brought out under the direction of Luther. One such—namely, Babst's Gesangbuch of 1545—has the melody, but set to another text.

(18) WACHET AUF, RUFT UNS DIE STIMME.

(From Nicolai's "Der Freuden Spiegel" of 1598.)

Wa - chet auf, ruft uns die Stim - - - - - me
Mit - ter - nacht heisst die - se Stun - - - - - de,

der Wäch - ter sehr hoch auf der Zin - ne,
sie ru - fen uns mit hel - lem Mun - de ;

wach auf, du Stadt Je - ru - sa - lem!
wo seid ihr klu - gen Jung - frau - en?

Wohl - auf, der

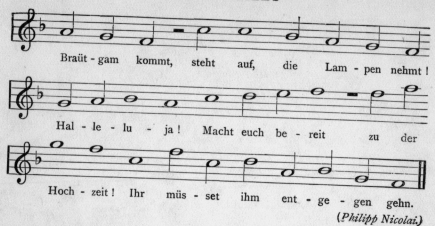

Braüt - gam kommt, steht auf, die Lam - pen nehmt!

Hal - le - lu - ja! Macht euch be - reit zu der

Hoch - zeit! Ihr müs - set ihm ent - ge - gen gehn.

(*Philipp Nicolai.*)

This " Hymn of the Voice at midnight, and the Wise Virgins who go to meet their Heavenly Bridegroom " was written by Philipp Nicolai, and appeared, with its magnificent tune, in the appendix to his religious treatise " Der Freuden Spiegel des ewigen Lebens " of 1598 (see p. 49, No. 11). The appendix contained four hymns and two tunes—the above and that of " Wie schön leuchtet der Morgenstern." The fact that these two tunes were noted, the other two being indicated by name only, suggests that the former were not known. Probably both of them, with the exception of the first two phrases of " Wie schön leuchtet," which are identical with those of an older melody, were composed by Philipp Nicolai himself.

(19) HERZLIEBSTER JESU, WAS HAST DU VERBROCHEN.

(Melody and figured Bass from the 1656 edition of Crüger's "Praxis Pietatis Melica.")

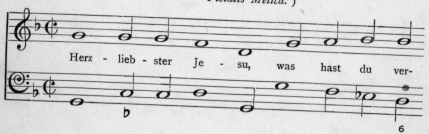

Herz - lieb - ster Je - su, was hast du ver-

6

bro - chen, dass man ein solch scharf Ur - teil hat

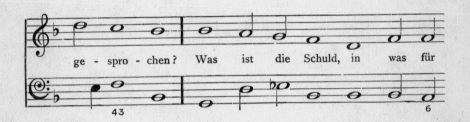

ge - spro - chen? Was ist die Schuld, in was für

Mis - se - tha - ten bist du ge - ra - ten?

(*Heermann.*)

The melody was composed by Johann Crüger, and first appeared in his " Newes vollkömliches Gesangbuch " of 1640, where it is harmonized for four voices. The above setting of the melody over a figured bass is from a copy of the 1656 edition of the " Praxis Pietatis Melica," belonging to the British Museum.

(20) WER NUR DEN LIEBEN GOTT LÄSST WALTEN.

(From Neumark's "Fortgepflanzter Lustwald" of 1657.)

Wer nur den lie - ben Gott lässt wal - ten und
Der wird ihn wun - der - lich er - hal - ten in

hof - fet auf ihn al - le - zeit, Wer Gott dem Al - ler-
al - ler Not und Trau - rig - keit.

höch - sten traut, der hat auf kei - nen Sand ge - baut.

(Neumark.)

Georg Neumark (1621-1681) published two books, containing both secular and sacred songs, with the fanciful titles " Lustwäldchen " (Little Pleasure-Grove) and " Fortgepflanzter Lustwald " (Transplanted Pleasure-Grove). The " Lustwäldchen " appeared in 1652, and the " Fortgepflantzer Lustwald " in 1657. The above text and melody, both of which were written by Neumark, occur in the latter, but not in the former. The author himself tells us that he wrote the text in 1641, but probably the melody was not composed till after 1652, as the hymn is not found in the " Lustwäldchen."

TRANSLATIONS OF THE GERMAN VERSES
GIVEN WITH THE MELODIES

(1) I. Christ is risen from all His sufferings: therefore should we all be glad: Christ will be our consolation. Kyrieleis. II. Were He not risen, the world would be lost. In that He is risen indeed, therefore praise we the Father of Jesus Christ. Kyrieleis. III. Halleluja! Therefore should we all be glad: Christ will be our consolation.

(2) Now pray we the Holy Ghost above all things to keep us in the true faith: that He may preserve us till the end of our life, when we shall depart home out of this misery. Kyrieleis.

(3) These are the holy Ten Commandments which the Lord our God gave us by His faithful servant Moses on the top of Mount Sinai. Kyrieleis.

(4) There is salvation hither come to us, purely out of grace and kindness. Works no longer avail; they cannot save us. The believer looks to Jesus Christ Who has made satisfaction for us all. He has become our mediator.

(5) Come, O God, Creator, Holy Spirit, visit the hearts of Thy people, fill them with Grace, for Thou knowest that they are of old Thy creation.

(6) Christ, who makes us holy, has committed no fault—He Who, for our sake, was taken like a thief in the night, brought before godless men, and falsely accused, mocked, derided and spat upon, as the scripture saith.

(7) (Secular) Insbruck, I must leave thee; I go my way into a foreign land. My joy is taken from me and I know not how to recover it when I am in exile.

(Sacred) O world, I must leave thee; I go my way into the everlasting Fatherland. My spirit will I resign; my body, too, and my life, will I place in the merciful hands of God.

(8) Our Father, which art in heaven, Thou Who bidst us all to be as brothers and to call upon Thy name and wouldst have us pray to Thee, grant that it be not the lips alone that pray; help us, so that the prayer may come from the ground of the heart.

(9) Through Adam's fall man's nature and state were wholly ruined. The same taint has descended to us, so that we could never have recovered without the consolation of God, Who has rescued us from the great injury which the serpent inflicted upon Eve, thereby bringing down upon itself God's wrath.

(10) Earnestly do I long for a holy death, for here I am compassed about with trouble and misery. I have a desire to depart from this evil world; I yearn for everlasting joys. Come quickly, Lord Jesus.

(11) Out of deep need I cry to Thee; Lord God, hear my call. Turn Thy gracious ear to me and open it unto my prayer. For if Thou wilt mark how many sins I have committed, who, Lord, may abide in Thy presence?

(12) In peace and joy I pass away at God's will. I am comforted in heart and mind, meek and tranquil. As God has promised me, death is only my falling to sleep.

(13) Rejoice now, dear Christian people, and let us break forth into joy, in that we have received consolation, and let us, one and all, sing with delight and love of what God has wrought in us, and of His great and marvellous work. Right dearly has He achieved it.

(14) O man, lament thy great sin, which caused Christ to proceed rom the bosom of His Father and come on earth. Of a maiden pure and gentle was He born, here for us, that He might be our mediator. To the dead He gave life and moreover banished all sickness; until the time drew nigh, when He should be offered up for us and should bear the heavy burden of our sins, yea, indeed, long upon the cross.

(15) Our God is a stronghold sure, a good defence and weapon. It is He who helps us to get free from all the distress that has now come upon us. The old enemy, the devil, is now in earnest: great power and much cunning are his gruesome armour; on earth there is no match for him.

(16) From high Heaven indeed come I hither; I bring you good news: of the good tidings which I bring in so great measure, of that will I sing and tell.

(17) To the one God on high be honour and thanks for His grace, by which now and for ever no harm can touch us. God has pleasure in us: now is there great peace without ceasing: all strife now has an end.

(18) Awake! The voice of the watchmen high up on the battlements is calling to us; awake, thou city of Jerusalem! It is the midnight hour: they call to us with clear voice, Where are ye, ye wise Virgins? Up! The Bridegroom comes! Arise! Take your lamps! Halleluja! Make ready for the marriage! Ye must go forth to meet Him.

(19) Beloved Jesu, what wrong hast Thou done that one should have pronounced so harsh a sentence? What is the offence? Into what kind of error hast Thou fallen?

(20) Whosoever lets the good God direct him and always sets his hope on Him, him will God wonderfully preserve in all distress and sadness. He who trusts in God the most highest, has not built upon the sand.

BILLING AND SONS, LTD., PRINTERS, GUILDFORD, ENGLAND

Recent Publications at the Faith Press.

SOLEMN TE DEUM IN B FLAT, for choir and congregation in unison, with an optional descant for boys' voices, by SYDNEY H. NICHOLSON. Price 6d. People's part, in ordinary notation and tonic sol-fa, price 1d., or 7s. 6d. per 100 (from the publishers only).

Specially written for the celebrations in thanksgiving for Peace.

A SIMPLE COMMUNION SERVICE IN G. By SYDNEY H. NICHOLSON, M.A., Organist and Master of the Choristers at Westminster Abbey. Third Impression. Price 8d.

The only service published which combines really good four-part harmony with simplicity.

MISSA L'HORA PASSA, for four voices, by LUDOVICO VIADANA (c. 1595). Adapted to English words by LIONEL SMITH, Choirmaster and Organist of St. Benet Fink, Tottenham. Price 1s. 4d.

This service is pre-eminently suitable as an introduction to the great polyphonic masses of the sixteenth-century masters : it is not beyond the scope of a good average parochial choir.

SHORT COMMUNION SERVICE IN E FLAT, by H. C. L. STOCKS, Organist of St. Asaph Cathedral. Price 8d.

REQUIEM MASS (for the English Rite) by THEO. KEYNES. Price 4d.

Written by request for churches where a good modern setting specially composed (not *adapted*) is desired for choir and organ at a requiem service.

THE TENOR TUNE BOOK, a collection of descants, ancient and modern, to well-known hymn tunes (other than plain chant) in which special care has been given to include only melodious faux-bourdons suitable for modern use. Quarter cloth boards. Second impression. Price 1s. 6d.

A SELECTION OF COMMUNIONS adapted from the Sarum Gradual by E. W. GOLDSMITH. Quarter cloth boards. Price 8d.

PLAIN-CHANT AND FABURDEN. By GODFREY SCEATS. A most interesting and readable introduction to the subject, with musical illustrations. Paper 6d.

MAGNIFICAT AND NUNC DIMITTIS, for solo voice and choir unaccompanied. By EDGAR T. COOK, Organist of Southwark Cathedral. Price 2d.

PRINTED AND PUBLISHED AT

THE FAITH PRESS

THE FAITH HOUSE, 22 BUCKINGHAM ST., CHARING CROSS, W.C. 2
MANCHESTER: 5 AND 7, GREENGATE, SALFORD.

Recent Publications at the Faith Press.

THE BIBLE AND THE DEAD. By the Rev. RALPH
CLAYTON, M.A. Price 2s. 6d.

"In determining what is the state of the departed, Mr. Clayton takes account
of the Bible, and that only. And he is careful to use the Bible scientifically, not
taking a 'proof text' here and a 'proof text' there, but ascertaining the gist of
Scripture teaching, and *what is implied* as well as what is stated."
—*Expository Times.*

CHURCH MUSIC. By SYDNEY NICHOLSON, M.A., Organist
and Master of the Choristers at Westminster Abbey. Price 2s. 6d.

The importance of this contribution is best illustrated by a
quotation from the introductory chapter:

"It cannot too often be emphasised that *not a note of music is
necessary to the performance of our Church services;* and it
follows that every note that is introduced must have some definite
and worthy purpose behind it. Far better no music at all than
music which has no justification."

THE LITTLE MISSAL FOR THE LAITY. Containing
the complete Communion Service as used by the Sacred Ministers,
the Canon being in Miles Coverdale's translation. With Collects,
Epistles, and Gospels from the Book of Common Prayer. Price
2s. and 2s. 6d.

PICTURES BY MR. T. NOYES LEWIS

1. **THE PLACE OF MEETING—at the Time of Communion.** A wonderful study of the warriors of all ages, seen
"Through the Veil" at a Solemn Requiem. Printed in colours,
on mount 22 in. × 16 in. Price 2s. 6d.

2. **THE STATIONS OF THE CROSS.** Fourteen magnificent cartoons of the Way of the Cross. Printed in Terracotta,
black and gold, after the best style of Greek vase paintings,
26 in. × 16 in. Price 14s. the set.

3. **THE THREE CROSS FLAG.** Four splendid colour
drawings of the Making of the Union Jack—St. George,
St. Andrew, and St. Patrick (each with his knight and his flag)
and Mother Church joining the three standards into one. Price
10s. 6d. the set.

PRINTED AND PUBLISHED AT

THE FAITH PRESS

THE FAITH HOUSE, 22 BUCKINGHAM ST., CHARING CROSS, W.C. 2
MANCHESTER: 5 AND 7, GREENGATE, SALFORD.

Recent Publications at the Faith Press.

RELIGIOUS COMMUNITIES OF THE CHURCH OF ENGLAND. By the Rev. A. T. CAMERON, M.A. With Preface by the Duke of Argyll. The only history of the revival of the religious life in England. Fully illustrated. Price 7s. 6d. net.

"No such complete handbook has ever yet been compiled."—*Church Times.*

"A book of absorbing interest."—*Scottish Chronicle.*

"A valuable footnote to English ecclesiastical history."—*Contemporary Review.*

"It will be a surprise to most people to read of the extent of the operations. . . . There is no doubt that the Bishops of the Church of England have shown great weakness."—*English Churchman.*

THE MYSTERY OF THE KINGDOM. An Historical and Critical Exposition of the Revelation of S. John the Divine. By the Rev. C. E. DOUGLAS, S.F. With 160 illustrations of ancient symbolism. Price 7s. 6d. net.

"An able investigation."—*The Times.*

"Cannot fail to throw a great deal of light on much that is obscure."—*Church Times.*

"Much of the material employed is new, especially in connection with the prophetic mysticism of the Hebrews, and is handled deftly and firmly throughout."—*Saturday Review.*

LINKS IN THE CHAIN OF RUSSIAN CHURCH HISTORY. By the Rev. Dr. FRERE, C.R. An account of the ancient patriarchate suspended by Tsar Peter and revived in 1917. Price 6s. net.

"A tonic against despair."—*Church Times.*

"Sure of the welcome which it undoubtedly deserves."—*Expository Times.*

PRIESTHOOD IN LITURGY AND LIFE. By the Rev. A. H. BAVERSTOCK, M.A. Price 3s. 6d. net.

"No priest will read it without profit, and it may be for many of them an introduction to ascetic theology, enlightening them on many subjects on which they were not only ignorant, but of the existence of which they were hardly aware. . . . It may be said, without exaggeration, that this book is thoroughly good all the way through."—*Church Times.*

THE LITURGY OF THE EASTERN ORTHODOX CHURCH. Translated with Notes by the Rev. H. HAMILTON MAUGHAN, M.A. With 11 full-page illustrations. Price 2s. 6d. net.

"The student and the advanced scholar will alike profit from this excellent work."—*Asiatic Review.*

"The very book for the reader who may desire to assist at the Liturgy in any of the Greek Churches in England. . . . Eleven full-page illustrations are of special interest, taken as they are from sources that usually are not accessible."—*Church Times.*

PRINTED AND PUBLISHED AT

THE FAITH PRESS

THE FAITH HOUSE, 22 BUCKINGHAM ST., CHARING CROSS, W.C 2

MANCHESTER: 5 AND 7, GREENGATE, SALFORD.